# PassKey EA Review Workbook

## Three Complete Enrolled Agent Practice Exams

## 2012-2013 Edition

**Authors:**
Collette Szymborski, CPA
Richard Gramkow, EA
Christy Pinheiro, EA ABA®

Passkey Publications
Elk Grove, CA

# Recent Praise for the PassKey EA Review Series

**Ralph P. Mendoza (Queens, New York)** This book did a great job of preparing me for the exam. I passed Part One on my first try.

**Michael Mirth (North Las Vegas, Nevada)**
The workbook is wonderful. I have timed myself to 3½ hours and have been able to complete each part in the time allowed. I believe I will pass the exam with no problems, and you can tell that the authors have a lot of experience in this field.

**Sung Hyon (Aurora, Colorado)**
Easy to understand and comprehensive. This book is one of the best EA review books I've found. I downloaded a sample PDF file from the publisher's website and liked how it read. I'd recommend this book.

**Chris Davidson (Orange County, California)**
I wanted to purchase a book with an easy writing style, so I could enjoy the process of preparing myself for the test. Text is bolded and bulleted to break the monotony. The examples (a big learning boost for me!) are completely enclosed in a box, so they clearly stand out. Each [unit] is followed by questions, complete with an explanation as to why the answer is correct. I showed the book to a CPA friend last night, and he went online immediately and ordered it! I HIGHLY recommend this book!

**Cynthia Adcock (Manchester, Tennessee)**
After using both the book and the audio book, I had no problems passing all three parts of the exam. It's a wonderful tool for anyone studying to become an Enrolled Agent.

**J. Lancaon (San Francisco, California)**
I passed all three parts of the EA exam! I have passed all parts of the EA exam using your book (thank you), and have recommended other coworkers use your book for their studying. The content of the tax material is right on point so that there were no surprises on the exams.

**M. Avila (Las Vegas, Nevada)**
This is a great low-cost study guide; I used it along with the IRS Pubs to pass. There are not many books available for this program at an affordable price.

**A. Engbretsen (Jacksonville, Florida)**
I purchased this item to use alongside classroom training that I am receiving. It has been so helpful, especially since I found out that the teacher uses the book to find his teaching material! Definitely recommend!

# Tammy the Tax Lady ®

Tammy the Tax Lady is a registered trademark of Passkey Publications

Editor: Cynthia Willett Sherwood, MSJ

*PassKey EA Review Workbook, Three Complete Enrolled Agent Practice Exams 2012-2013 Edition*

ISBN978-1-935664-18-5

First Printing. PassKey EA Review
PassKey EA Review® is a U.S. Registered Trademark



PassKey Publications, PO Box 580465, Elk Grove, CA 95758

www.PassKeyPublications.com

# Table of Contents

# Introduction

Welcome to the PassKey EA Exam Review Workbook. This workbook is designed to be an additional study tool to your existing study guide. It is not designed as a "stand alone" workbook, although you will not be required to refer back to the PassKey study guides in order to use this book. The test questions are all unique, and not found in the PassKey study guides. This is intentional—so candidates can have a more true-to-life test-taking experience when they go through the workbook questions.

Any EA exam candidate will benefit from the exam questions and detailed answers in this workbook. We suggest that you use this workbook to prepare for the exam in a realistic setting. Set aside an uninterrupted time block and test yourself just the way you would if you were actually taking the EA exam at a testing center.

Score yourself at the end, and go through the answers carefully. Unlike the Prometric exam, you will have a complete, clear answer for all the questions. If you miss a question, you will know why. Use this workbook to find your weak points and concentrate on those. You should have at least 70% correct. Any score below 70% means that you probably need to study more.

This workbook is designed for the 2012-2013 testing season that lasts through February 28, 2013. All of the questions are based on 2011 tax law until the current exam is retired. If you have any questions about the actual exam, or if you want to sign up for it, call Prometric directly at 1-800-306-3926.

If you wish to find out more about the Complete Enrolled Agent study guides and other books by PassKey Publications visit our website at *www.PassKeyPublications.com.*

Successfully passing the EA Exam can launch you into a fulfilling and lucrative new career. The exam requires intense preparation and diligence, but with the help of PassKey's EA Review, you will have the tools you need to learn how to become an Enrolled Agent. As the authors of the PassKey EA Review, we wish you much success.

Good luck on your exam!

# Nine Steps for the IRS EA Exam

**STEP 1-Learn**

Learn about the Enrolled Agent designation. An Enrolled Agent (EA) has passed a three-part test covering all aspects of federal taxation and has passed an IRS background check. As a result, an EA can represent people before the Internal Revenue Service, just like attorneys and CPAs.

**STEP 2-Gather information**

Gather information about the Special Enrollment Examination. The IRS publishes basic information about becoming an Enrolled Agent on the Enrollment Overview page of its website. Additionally, candidates will find important information about registering, scheduling, fees, and the format of the EA Exam from the Prometric/IRS website. Prometric administers the Special Enrollment Exam on behalf of the IRS. Candidates will want to download the *"Enrolled Agent Candidate Information Bulletin"* from the Prometric site.

**STEP 3-Sign up with Prometric**

Sign up to take the Special Enrollment Examination. The easiest way is to sign up online. Candidates sign up for the test using IRS Form 2587 or by using the online Form 2587 found on the Prometric/IRS website. The online form is easier and more secure. The fee is $101 for each part of the exam.

**STEP 4-Choose a test site**

Choose a test site and test date with Prometric. There are test sites throughout the United States and all over the world. Choose a site that's convenient for you.

**STEP 5-Adopt a study plan**

Adopt a study plan that covers all the tax topics on the Special Enrollment Examination. Approach each study unit at a pace of three to four hours each. A good rule of thumb is to study at least 60 hours for each of the three exam sections, committing at least 15 hours per week. Start well in advance of the exam date. There's absolutely no point in cramming at the last minute, especially for a test covering something as hard as taxation. Take your time. Try focusing on the "big picture," especially in areas of taxation that might be new to you.

**STEP 6-Get plenty of rest, exercise, and good nutrition**

Get plenty of rest, exercise, and good nutrition in the two weeks before the EA exam. Don't focus on studying. Instead, review your notes to get an overall feel for the main points of the test. Don't cram in the last two weeks. It will prove counterproductive.

**STEP 7-Test day has arrived!**

On test day, don't forget your driver's license, ID, or passport! Arrive early to the test site, sign in, and get situated. Have breakfast or lunch, and go to the bathroom before entering to take the exam, because any breaks you take will cut into your exam time. Although you will be able to leave the test center to go to the restroom or take a quick break, the clock does not stop on the exam. You won't be able to bring anything into the test room except glasses and an ID, so make sure you eat and go to the bathroom BEFORE the test. If you need accommodations for a medical condition or a disability, call the test site in advance. The testing site will give each candidate scratch paper, pencils, and a calculator. A candidate cannot bring his or her own paper or calculator.

**STEP 8-During the exam**

During the exam, do not speak with other students or you may be asked to leave the testing center. Also, with the computer-based test format, the exam questions may differ slightly from what other test-takers have seen. Don't fuss over one question. If you are unsure, just guess and move on! You can always go back at the end if you have time. The exam will allow you to review all your answers if you have time left over. Your scores will be available immediately after the exam. Candidates are not penalized additional points for wrong answers, so it is better to answer every question rather than leave one blank.

**Step 9-Congratulations! You passed!**

Now you must begin the process of applying for your EA designation through the IRS. You must submit your application fee and IRS Form 23 to the IRS in order to become an Enrolled Agent. Each application is examined by the IRS and each applicant is investigated for suitability. This process takes about three months.

Exam candidates can download IRS **Form 23** at *www.IRS.gov*. Incomplete applications will not be processed. The most common delays are due to:

- Lack of an original signature on IRS Form 23 (NO PHOTOCOPIES)
- Unsigned check for the application fee
- Missing application fee
- Incomplete or unfinished applications

***Note:** Although it is not required, it is easier for the IRS to process your Enrolled Agent application (**Form 23**) if you include copies of your Prometric score reports. Candidates who do so tend to get their applications processed much faster.

After the application is processed, the IRS will issue you a Treasury Card. Once you have your Treasury Card and your enrollment number, you are officially an Enrolled Agent!

# Essential Tax Figures for 2011

# (for Part 1: Individuals)

Listed in this beginning section are the most common figures you will see on the IRS Enrolled Agent exam. Although you do not have to memorize exact figures most of the time, the following basic figures are necessary and you should know them.

Below is a quick summary of all the essential tax figures affecting individual taxpayers for tax year 2011:

**Income Tax Return Filing Deadline:** April 17, 2012 (due date for tax returns and extensions)[1]

**The Personal Exemption:** $3,700 (increased from 2010)
***Note:** In 2011, the personal exemption and itemized deductions do NOT phase out at higher income levels, as in previous years.

**2011 Social Security Taxable Wage Base:** $106,800

**2011 Medicare Taxable Wage Base:** No limit

**The Annual Gift Tax Exclusion:** $13,000 (unchanged from 2010)

**2011 Standard Deduction Amounts**

- Married Filing Jointly (or Qualifying Widow/Widower) $11,600
- Head of Household $8,500
- Single $5,800
- Married Filing Separately $5,800
- Dependents $950
- Blind taxpayers and senior citizens (over 65) qualify for an increased standard deduction. Additional amounts for 2011 (per taxpayer) are:
    - $1,450 for Single or Head of Household
    - $1,150 for Married Filing Jointly, Married Filing Separately, or Qualifying Widow.

**Section 179 Expense:** $500,000 of qualified expenditures/phase-out at $2 million

---

[1] Note that the *normal* filing deadline for individual returns is April 15. However, April 15, 2012 is a Sunday and April 16, 2012 falls on Emancipation Day, which is a federal holiday in the District of Columbia (Washington, D.C.)

**Mileage Rates 2011**

- **Business Miles**
  - Before 7/1/2011: 51 cents per mile
  - After 6/30/2011: 55.5 cents per mile
- **Medical or Moving Miles**
  - Before 7/1/2011: 19 cents per mile
  - After 6/30/2011: 23.5 cents per mile
- 14 cents per mile for charitable purposes (unchanged from 2010)

**Retirement Plan Contribution Limits For 2011:** Traditional or Roth IRA: $5,000 ($6,000 for taxpayers age 50 and over)

**2011 Roth IRA Phase-Out AGI limits**

- Married Filing Jointly: $169,000 to $179,000
- Single or Head of Household: $107,000 to $122,000
- Married Filing Separately: $0 to $10,000

**Tax Year 2011 Earned Income Tax Credit (EITC) Income Thresholds**
Earned Income and adjusted gross income (AGI) must each be less than:

- $43,998 ($49,078 MFJ) with three or more qualifying children
- $40,964 ($46,044 MFJ) with two qualifying children
- $36,052 ($41,132 MFJ) with one qualifying child
- $13,660 ($18,740 MFJ) with no qualifying children

**Tax Year 2011 Maximum EITC Credit:**

- $5,751 with three or more qualifying children
- $5,112 with two qualifying children
- $3,094 with one qualifying child
- $464 with no qualifying children

Investment income must be $3,150 **or less** for the year in order to qualify for the EITC.

The **Adoption Credit** is refundable in 2011: $13,360 (maximum credit)

**2011 Education Credits and Deductions**

- The American Opportunity Credit is a maximum annual credit of $2,500 per student.
- The Lifetime Learning Credit is a maximum of $2,000 per return.
- The Tuition and Fees Deduction is a maximum of $4,000 in 2011.
- The Student Loan Interest Deduction is a maximum $2,500 of qualified loan interest paid in 2011.

# New Tax Law Affecting Individuals for 2011

# (For Part 1: Individuals)

**Adoption Credit:** In 2011, as in 2010, the Adoption Credit is refundable. This provision expires in 2012. The maximum Adoption Credit is $13,360 in 2011. Taxpayers who adopt a "special needs" child may claim the credit, even if they have no adoption expenses.

**Advance EITC:** Starting in 2011, Advance EITC is no longer available.[2]

**Alternative Minimum Tax (AMT):** The AMT exemption amount in 2011 has increased to $48,450 ($74,450 if Married Filing Jointly or a Qualifying Widow(er); $37,225 if Married Filing Separately).

**Capital Gains and Losses:** Effective in 2011, capital gains and losses are no longer reported directly on Schedule D. The IRS has introduced the new Form 8949, *Sales and Other Dispositions of Capital Assets*. This form is used to list all capital gain and loss transactions; the subtotals are then carried over to Schedule D.

**Due Date:** The due date for 2011 tax returns is April 17, 2012. The customary tax filing deadline is April 15, 2012, but this is a Sunday and April 16, 2012 falls on Emancipation Day in the District of Columbia (Washington D.C.)

**EITC Penalty Increased:** There is a $500 penalty for each failure to comply with EITC due diligence requirements. The penalty was increased from $100 to $500 per return. Preparers are also now required to fill out and attach Form 8867, *Paid Preparers Earned Income Credit Checklist*.

**E-File Mandate:** A new law requires most tax preparers to e-file income tax returns prepared and filed for individuals, trusts, and estates. The mandate applies to any paid preparer who anticipates filing 11 or more Forms 1040 and/or 1041 during the year. Business and payroll tax returns are not included in this mandate.

**Health Savings Accounts (HSAs) and Archer MSAs:** The additional tax on distributions from HSAs and Archer MSAs not used for qualified medical expenses increased to 20%. Beginning in 2011, only drugs that are prescribed by a doctor

---

[2]The Education Jobs and Medicaid Assistance Act of 2010 permanently repealed the Advance EITC.

(including insulin) are qualified medical expenses. Over-the-counter medications no longer qualify.

**Mandatory EFTPS:** Businesses must make deposits using the Electronic Federal Tax Payment System (EFTPS); Federal Deposit Coupons are no longer an option. Small businesses that have less than $2,500 in quarterly tax liabilities can choose to pay using a paper check when they file their quarterly returns.

**Mandatory PTIN:** Starting in 2011, all paid preparers are required to have a Preparer Tax Identification Number (PTIN) before preparing returns.

**SE Health Insurance:** The SE Health Insurance deduction no longer offsets SE Tax, as it did in 2010. In 2011, it is allowed only as an above-the-line deduction on Page 1 of **Form 1040**.

**Self-Employment and Payroll Tax Changes:** 2011 saw a temporary decrease in the employee's share of payroll tax. Social Security was withheld from wages at the rate of 4.2%(down from 6.2%). In 2011, there was no change to Medicare withholding. The same reduction applies to net earnings from self-employment—the temporary rate was 10.4% (down from 12.4%), up to the Social Security wage limit of $106,800. As a result of this change, the overall self-employment tax was reduced from 15.3% to 13.3%.

**Standard Mileage Rate:** In 2011, the standard mileage rate may be used by a vehicle used for hire, such as a shuttle or a taxicab.

**Energy Credits:** There are changes to the Non-business Energy Property Credit for tax year 2011; the amounts are less than what was allowed in previous years.

**Health Coverage Tax Credit (HCTC):**This is a refundable credit that pays 72.5% of qualified health insurance premiums for eligible individuals and their families. In 2011, there is an additional 7.5% retroactive credit.

**Estate Tax:** For 2011, the estate tax has been reinstated, and the combined exclusion for estate and gift tax is $5 million. A new provision in 2011 allows for "portability" where a predeceased spouse's unused estate tax exclusion may be transferred to the surviving spouse.

# New Rules for Businesses 2011 Tax Year

# (for Part 2: Businesses)

**Income Tax Return Filing Deadline:** April 17, 2012 (due date for individual and partnership tax returns and extensions)[3]

**2011 Social Security Taxable Wage Base:** $106,800. In 2011, the Social Security portion of the FICA tax for employees ONLY is reduced from 6.2% to 4.2%. The employer's portion of Social Security remains at 6.2%. The Social Security tax rate for self-employed persons is similarly reduced, from 12.4% to 10.4%.

**2011 Medicare Taxable Wage Base:** No limit

**Section 179 Expense:** $500,000 of qualified expenditures/phase-out at $2 million. The special Section 179 deduction for qualified leasehold improvements was extended for the 2011 tax year.

**100% Bonus Depreciation Extended:** A special 100% depreciation allowance has been extended through 2011. In order to qualify for bonus depreciation, the property must be new (cannot be used) and must generally be MACRS property with a recovery period of 20 years or less.

**Mileage Rates 2011**

- Business Miles
    - Before 7/1/2011: 51 cents per mile
    - After 6/30/2011: 55.5 cents per mile
- Medical or Moving Miles
    - Before 7/1/2011: 19 cents per mile
    - After 6/30/2011: 23.5 cents per mile
- 14 cents per mile for charitable purposes (unchanged from 2010)

**Retirement Plan Contribution Limits For 2011:** Traditional or Roth IRA: $5,000 ($6,000 for taxpayers age 50 and over)

---

[3] Note that the *normal* filing deadline for individual returns is April 15. However, April 15, 2012 is a Sunday and April 16, 2012 falls on Emancipation Day, which is a federal holiday in the District of Columbia (Washington, D.C.)

# New Business Regulations For 2011

**Basis Reporting:** Brokers are required to report basis information on **Form 1099-B** starting in 2011. The information must also include whether the holding period is short-term or long-term.

**Cafeteria Plans:** A new safe harbor exception to the non-discrimination requirements for cafeteria plans is available (covered later under employer-offered retirement plans).

**Corporate Tax Returns:** In 2011, the corporate **Schedule A,** *Cost of Goods Sold,* and **Schedule E,** *Compensation of Officers*, are replaced with the new **Form 1125-A**, *Cost of Goods Sold*, and **Form 1125-E**, *Compensation of Officers*, which are attached to **Form 1120** (for C Corporations) or **Form 1120S** (for S Corporations).

**Electronic Filing Mandate:** Paid preparers who prepare 11 or more individual or trust tax returns in 2012 (for the 2011 tax year) are required to e-file.

**Estate and Gift Tax:** The estate tax has been reinstated for 2011 and is unified with the gift tax. The exclusion for estate and gift tax is $5 million.

**Federal Deposit Coupons:** As of January 1, 2011, businesses and individuals may no longer use Federal Deposit Coupons to make federal tax deposits. All deposits must be made electronically using EFTPS. There is an exception for very small businesses that have less than $2,500 in quarterly tax liabilities. These businesses may pay their liabilities using a paper check when they file their quarterly returns.

**Form 1099-K:** The new IRS **Form 1099-K**, *Merchant Card and Third Party Payments*, is used to report the gross proceeds of credit card and third party network transactions made to taxpayers. Businesses may receive Form 1099-K if they accepted merchant cards for payments or because they received payments through a third party network that exceeded $20,000 in gross total reportable payment transactions, and the total number of those transactions exceeded 200 for the calendar year.

**FUTA:** The Federal Unemployment Tax (FUTA) tax rate is 6.0% in 2011. FUTA tax is a tax imposed on the employer (not the employee) for the first $7,000 in wages paid to each employee during the year.

**General Business Credits:** All General Business Credits (including carry-forwards and carrybacks) are now reported on **Form 3800**, *General Business Credit*.

**Health Savings Accounts:** The tax on distributions from Health Savings Accounts (HSAs) and Archer MSAs that are not used for qualified medical expenses has increased to 20% for tax year 2011.

**Household Employees:** For 2011, the Social Security and Medicare wage threshold for household employees remains unchanged at $1,700. This means that taxpayers who paid a household employee cash wages of less than $1,700 in 2011 do not have to report and pay Social Security and Medicare taxes on that employee's 2011 wages.

**Partnership Tax Returns:** In 2011, the partnership **Schedule A**, *Cost of Goods Sold*, is also replaced with **Form 1125-A**, and should be attached to **Form 1065**.

**S Corporation Built-In Gains Tax (the "BIG TAX"):** The American Recovery and Reinvestment Act of 2009 modified recognition period from ten to seven years for certain S Corporation's taxable years. In 2011, the recognition period was reduced even further from seven to five years, beginning with the first day of the first taxable year that the corporation was an S Corporation.

**Self-Employed Health Insurance Deduction REPEALED:** This deduction was repealed in 2011, and is no longer allowed on Schedule SE as a reduction against self-employment tax. The deduction is still allowed as an adjustment to income for self-employed taxpayers.

**Start-up Expenses:** The amount that can be claimed as start-up expenses for businesses in 2011 is $5,000 (down from $10,000 in 2010). The deduction is reduced dollar for dollar for any start-up costs that exceed $50,000. Any remaining start-up costs can be amortized using the straight-line method over 180 months.

**Work Opportunity Credit:** On November 21, 2011, President Obama signed into law the Vow to Hire Heroes Act of 2011, which amends and expands the definition of WOTC's veteran target groups. The changes and new provisions in this act apply to individuals who begin to work for an employer the day after its enactment, November 22, 2011, and before January 1, 2013. Employers may be eligible for a tax credit of up to $5,600 per employee if they hire a qualified veteran.

# New Tax Preparer Ethics Regulations For 2011

# (for Part 3: Representation)

**Circular 230 Update:** Treasury Department Circular 230 now applies to ALL paid preparers.[4] The new ethics regulations affect:

- Individuals who practice before the IRS
- The new designation of "Registered Tax Return Preparer" (RTRP)
- Providers of continuing education programs

**Mandatory PTIN Requirement:** Beginning January 1, 2011 all paid preparers were required to have a Preparer Tax Identification Number (PTIN) *before* preparing returns.

**Mandatory E-filing:** Tax preparers must register for an EFIN (Electronic Filing Identification Number) if they plan to e-file tax returns and reasonably expect to file 11 or more Forms 1040, 1040A, 1040EZ, or 1041 during 2012. Tax preparers may request a waiver of the e-file mandate.

**Paper Filed Returns:** Tax returns prepared by a paid preparer but filed on paper must be submitted with **Form 8948**, *Preparer Explanation for Not Filing Electronically.* A reason must be provided for each return that is not e-filed. Tax return preparers may request an undue hardship waiver from the e-file requirement using **Form 8944**, *Preparer e-file Hardship Waiver Request.*

**Disreputable Conduct Expanded:** The definition of "disreputable conduct" has been expanded and now includes:

- Willfully failing to e-file returns electronically if they fall under the e-filing mandate, and
- Failing to include a valid PTIN on tax returns.

**EITC Due Diligence Penalty Increased:** Paid preparers failing to meet their due diligence requirements on Earned Income Tax Credit (EITC) claims face higher penalties for returns required to be filed after December 31, 2011. The penalty increased from $100 to $500 per return.

---

[4]The final regulations, TD 9527, were released in June 2011.

**EITC Returns Must be Submitted with Form 8867:** Tax preparers must complete and attach **Form 8867**, *Paid Preparer's Earned Income Credit Checklist*, and submit the form with all EITC refund claims.

**Equitable Relief:** Requests for Equitable Relief are no longer required to be submitted within two years of IRS collection activity.

**Registered Tax Return Preparer (RTRP):** Circular 230 explains the new designation of "Registered Tax Return Preparers," including their exam and CPE requirements. Individuals who are required to take the RTRP competency test will have until December 31, 2013 to pass the test.

**New Preparer Education Requirements:** Paid preparers who are not attorneys, Certified Public Accountants, Enrolled Agents, Enrolled Actuaries, or Enrolled Retirement Plan Agents will be required to complete 15 hours of continuing education annually. The 15 hours include three hours of federal tax law, two hours of ethics, and 10 hours of other federal tax law topics.

# Part 1: Individuals Practice Exam

**Test tip!** Time yourself. Set up a watch or other digital timer while you read and answer the questions. You will have 3.5 hours to take the EA exam, with approximately two minutes to answer each question. Do not spend an inordinate amount of time on any one question. Don't run out of time! It's the number one reason why first-time test takers fail.

1. Youssef purchased his home six years ago for $175,000. Many months ago, he lost his job and was no longer able to make his mortgage payments. On July 1, 2011, Youssef moved out of the home to live with relatives. On August 30, 2011, the bank foreclosed on the home. On December 15, 2011, the bank discontinued its collection activity and canceled the remaining debt. The fair market value at the time of foreclosure was $100,000 because of the poor housing market, but Youssef still owed $150,000 on the mortgage. None of the loan proceeds were used for any purpose other than to buy, build, or substantially improve the principal residence. Youssef never used the home for business or rental purposes and has not filed for bankruptcy. Based on this information, how should Youssef report this transaction?

A. Youssef should include the debt cancellation amount in income, on Line 21 of his **Form 1040.**

B. Youssef should report a long-term capital loss of $50,000 on **Schedule D**.

C. Youssef should report $50,000 of canceled debt on **Form 982,** and the canceled debt will NOT be taxable to Youssef.

D. Youssef does not have to report this transaction on his tax return.

2.Which of the following scenarios is considered a passive activity and subject to the passive activity rules?

A. Rental activity in which the taxpayer is a real estate professional.

B. Farming activity in which the taxpayer does not materially participate.

C. A general partner who earns income from the partnership.

D. Income earned from investments.

3. Felicia has a part-time nanny that works in her home. She pays the nanny $1,600 in wages during 2011. Which of the following statements is TRUE?

A. Felicia does not have to report and pay Social Security and Medicare taxes on the nanny's 2011 wages.

B. The income is not taxable to the nanny.

C. No reporting is required by either party if the wages are paid in cash.

D. Felicia can deduct the nanny's wages on a **Schedule C-EZ**.

4. Wesley has a fair amount of employee business expenses this year. In which scenario would he use **Form 2106** for his expenses?

A. When Wesley has no records of the expenses.

B. When Wesley's employer reimburses the full amount of Wesley's expenses.

C. When Wesley's expense reimbursements from his employer were included in his wage income.

D. When Wesley chooses not to deduct his employee business expenses.

5. Which of the following numbers is NOT a valid Taxpayer Identification Number (TIN)?

A. ATIN.

B. ITIN.

C. SSN.

D. PTIN.

6. What is the maximum amount of investment income that can be earned by a dependent child in2011 without triggering the "Kiddie Tax"?

A. $500.

B. $950.

C. $1,900.

D. $5,700.

7. Jim worked for a construction company in 2011. In November, the owner of the company filed bankruptcy and disappeared. Jim never received his **Form W-2**. What form must he use instead?

A. Form 1099-MISC.

B. Form 2848.

C. Form 4852.

D. Form W-7.

8. How are gambling losses deducted on an individual tax return?

A. As an adjustment to income on **Form 1040**.

B. As an itemized deduction NOT subject to the 2% floor on **Schedule A**.

C. As an itemized deduction subject to the 2% floor on **Schedule A.**

D. Gambling losses are never deductible.

9. A taxpayer is blind and has a service dog (a seeing-eye dog for the blind). The taxpayer works full-time and makes $50,000 per year. Which of the following statements is TRUE?

A. The veterinary care for the service animal is deductible as a medical expense.

B. The veterinary care for the service animal is NOT deductible as a medical expense.

C. This blind person is able to work and is therefore not considered "disabled" for tax purposes, meaning he cannot claim medical expenses related to his condition.

D. Veterinary care is never deductible as a personal or medical expense.

10. Reggie has arthritis and a heart condition. He cannot climb stairs or get into a bathtub. On his doctor's advice, he installs a bathroom with a shower stall on the first floor of the two-story house that he rents. Although the landlord allowed the improvements, she did not pay any of the cost of buying and installing the special plumbing and did not lower the rent. Which of the following statements is true?

A. Reggie can include in medical expenses the entire amount he paid.

B. Reggie cannot deduct any of the expenses as a medical expense because he does not own the property.

C. Reggie cannot deduct any of the expenses because none was for the actual treatment of a medical condition.

D. Reggie can deduct a portion of the expenses, based on the overall square footage of the home.

11. Gary is unmarried. Gary's mother, for whom he can claim a dependency exemption, lived in an apartment by herself. She died on September 2, 2011. The cost of the upkeep of her apartment for the year until her death was $6,000. Gary paid $4,000 and his brother paid $2,000. His brother made no other payments toward his mother's support. His mother had no income. Which of the following statements is TRUE?

A. Gary cannot claim his mother as a dependent, but he may claim Head of Household filing status.

B. Gary may not claim Head of Household filing status, but he may still claim his mother as a dependent.

C. Gary may claim his mother as a dependent, and he may also claim Head of Household filing status.

D. Gary cannot claim Head of Household filing status, and he cannot claim his mother as a dependent.

12. In 2011 Regina, who is single and lives alone, gives birth to a baby boy, but he only lives for two days. Regina did not get a Social Security Number issued for the child. Which of the following statements is TRUE?

A. Regina may not claim the child as a dependent because he did not live with her for at least six months.

B. Regina may not claim the child as a dependent because he did not live with her for at least six months; however, Regina still qualifies for Head of Household filing status.

C. Regina may claim the child as a dependent and may file as Head of Household since she is unmarried.

D. Regina may claim the child as a dependent, but she may not file as Head of Household because she did not maintain a home for a qualifying dependent for at least six months.

13. Rodrigo provides all the financial support for his father, who is a citizen of Mexico. His father is not eligible for a Social Security Number. Rodrigo wants to claim his father as a dependent on his tax return. What must he do?

A. Nothing. Rodrigo cannot claim a citizen of Mexico on his tax return.

B. His father must apply for an Individual Taxpayer Identification Number (ITIN), and then Rodrigo can claim his father as a dependent.

C. Rodrigo can file a paper return and attach a copy of his father's identification in lieu of a Taxpayer Identification Number.

D. Rodrigo must apply for a Social Security Number on behalf of his father, before he can claim his father on a tax return.

14. Which of the following is TRUE about Roth retirement accounts?

A. In 2011, anyone can make a qualified rollover contribution to a Roth IRA regardless of the taxpayer's modified AGI.

B. In 2011, anyone can participate in and contribute to a Roth IRA regardless of the amount of the taxpayer's modified AGI.

C. In 2011, anyone withdrawing funds from a Roth IRA will be subject to a withdrawal penalty, unless that person is over 59½ when the withdrawal is made.

D. In 2011, taxpayers can contribute to a traditional IRA as well as a Roth IRA, regardless of the taxpayer's modified AGI.

15. Abel's personal-use car was damaged in a flood in 2011. Abel's loss after insurance reimbursement was $2,000. His adjusted gross income in 2011 is $29,500. Abel must first apply the $100 rule and then the 10% rule. What is Abel's deductible casualty loss in 2011?

A. $0.

B. $1,900.

C. $2,000.

D. $2,950.

16. Sandy's unmarried son, Greg, lived with her all year. Greg was 26 years old at the end of the year and his gross income was $5,000. Greg is not disabled. Sandy paid all the costs of keeping up the home. Can Sandy claim Greg as a dependent and also file as Head of Household?

A. Sandy can claim Greg as a dependent and also claim Head of Household filing status.

B. Sandy can claim Greg as a dependent, but she cannot claim Head of Household filing status.

C. Sandy cannot claim Greg as a dependent, but she can file as Head of Household.

D. Sandy cannot claim Greg as a dependent, and she does not qualify for Head of Household filing status.

17. John and Dianne are married, but have been legally separated since April 2011. They have one daughter, Simone, who lived with Dianne all year. Dianne provided over half of Simone's support. John does not want to file jointly with Dianne. What is the best filing status for Dianne?

A. Single.

B. Head of Household.

C. Married Filing Separately.

D. Married Filing Jointly.

18. Daniel and Maria are married and file jointly. They do not have any children. However, Daniel supports his 65-year-old stepmother, who lives in an assisted living facility. Daniel's stepmother has interest income of $2,300 in 2011, and no other income. How many exemptions may Daniel and Maria claim on their tax return?

A. 0.

B. 1.

C. 2.

D. 3.

19. Odin and Suzy have been physically separated since September2011, but they are not divorced. Their 14-year-old son, Sam, lived with Odin the rest of the year. Odin provided over half the cost of keeping up his home. Odin plans to file Married Filing Separately, and he also plans to itemize his deductions. Suzy does not have any dependents. What are Suzy's options?

A. Suzy may file Head of Household, so long as she doesn't take the dependency exemption for Sam.

B. Suzy must file MFS, and she may itemize or take the standard deduction.

C. Suzy can file Head of Household, so long as she lives with her husband the last six months of the year.

D. Suzy must file MFS, and she will also be forced to itemize. She cannot claim the dependency exemption for Sam.

20. Each of the following individuals will automatically be taxed as a resident of the United States EXCEPT:

A. A foreign-born individual physically present in the United States for 350 days.

B. A non-resident alien who marries a U.S. citizen in 2011.

C. A foreign-born person with a valid green card.

D. A foreign-born green card holder living outside the United States for one year.

21. Harold lives with his 17-year-old son Chad. Harold provided $5,000 toward Chad's support for the year. Chad also has a part-time job and provided $15,000 toward his own support. Can Harold claim his son as a dependent?

A. Yes, Harold can claim his son as a qualifying child, because he is a minor.

B. Yes, Harold can claim Chad as a qualifying relative.

C. No, Chad provided more than half of his own support for the year. Therefore, he is not Harold's qualifying child or his qualifying relative.

D. None of the above.

22. Greta has four dependents. Which of the following dependents would qualify for the Child Tax Credit?

A. Max, 21 years old and a full-time college student.

B. Becca, 18 years old and disabled.

C. Aaron, 16 years old and a full-time student.

D. Susannah, 65 years old, Greta's dependent parent.

23. For the purposes of the Earned Income Credit, which of the following types of income does NOT qualify as "earned income" in order to claim the EIC?

A. Non-taxable combat pay.

B. Union strike benefits.

C. Tips.

D. Legal gambling income.

24. Desmond has a dependent child who is 15 years old. Desmond is single and qualifies for Head of Household filing status. In 2011, his income was $22,000 in wages and he also had investment income. What is the maximum amount of investment income that Desmond can have before he is disqualified from claiming the Earned Income Credit (EIC)?

A. $950.

B. $2,900.

C. $3,150.

D. $5,700.

25. Ray pays $500 a month for after-school care for his daughter Melanie. On May 1, Melanie turned 13. How much of Ray's expenses are qualifying expenses for the purposes of the Child and Dependent Care Credit?

A. $2,000.

B. $3,000.

C. $6,000.

D. Some other amount.

26. Which of the following persons can claim the Earned Income Tax Credit?

A. A taxpayer with a valid Social Security Number and a foster child.

B. A disabled taxpayer who is a dependent of another person.

C. A taxpayer with a qualifying child, who is filing Married Filing Separately.

D. A 66-year-old single taxpayer who meets the income thresholds, but does not have a qualifying child.

27. Francesca and Bob were legally married for three years. In 2011, Francesca moves out and files for an annulment. However, the annulment is not final until February 10, 2012. They do not have any dependents. What is Francesca's filing status for 2011?

A. Single.

B. Married Filing Separately.

C. Married Filing Jointly.

D. Head of Household.

28. Eligible educators can deduct up to a maximum of ______ in qualified expenses paid in 2011 as an adjustment to income.

A. $0.

B. $150.

C. $250.

D. $500.

29. Rebecca works as a real estate agent for Big House Real Estate Company. She visits Big House's offices at least once a day to check her mail and her messages. She manages dozens of listings and splits her real estate commissions with Big House. She does not work for any other real estate company. How must Rebecca be classified by her employer?

A. Employee.

B. Statutory employee.

C. Corporate shareholder.

D. Statutory non-employee.

30. In 2011, what is the maximum amount of wages subject to Social Security tax?

A. There is no maximum.

B. $86,000.

C. $102,800.

D. $106,800.

31. Divorce decrees may define alimony payments. However, when may the IRS reclassify alimony payments as child support?

A. If the alimony payments are to a non-resident alien spouse.

B. If the alimony payments are decreased because of a contingency related to the child.

C. If one spouse refuses to cash the alimony checks.

D. If one spouse contests a prenuptial agreement.

32. Which of the following credits is a REFUNDABLE tax credit?

A. The Dependent Care Credit.

B. The Lifetime Learning Credit.

C. Credit for the Elderly or the Disabled.

D. The Adoption Credit.

33. Melissa had a very difficult year financially. In 2011, she stopped paying her credit card bills and other obligations, and she received a 1099-C reporting canceled debt. In which case must canceled debt be included in Melissa's gross income?

A. If the debt was discharged before Melissa filed for bankruptcy.

B. If Melissa was insolvent at the time of cancellation.

C. If the cancellation is qualified principal residence debt.

D. If the canceled debt was forgiven as a gift from a family member.

34. Raul had the following income items in 2011. Which of the following amounts is not considered taxable income?

A. $20,000 in wages.

B. $12,000 inheritance.

C. $2,500 in traditional IRA distributions.

D. $3,000 in alimony.

35. Tina is unmarried. Tina and her 5-year-old son Bradley lived all year with her mother, Marsha, who paid the entire cost of keeping up the home. Tina's AGI is $19,000. Marsha's AGI is $28,000. Tina and Marsha both attempt to claim Bradley as a qualifying child for the Earned Income Credit. What is the "tie-breaker rule" regarding this scenario?

A. Neither can claim Bradley as a qualifying child.

B. Marsha has the higher AGI and also paid the cost of keeping up the home, so she has the right to claim Bradley as her dependent, as well as to file as Head of Household.

C. Tina has the right to claim Bradley as her qualifying child, because she is the child's parent.

D. Tina has the right to file as Head of Household, as well as claim Bradley as her qualifying child.

36. Emily and Steve are divorced. They have one child who is 13 years old. The child lives with Emily most of the time and stays with Steve on weekends. Emily has primary custody. If Steve receives permission from Emily, the custodial parent, to claim the child on his tax return, is Steve eligible for the Earned Income Credit based on the dependent child?

A. Yes.

B. No.

C. Only if Steve provides over half of his child's overall support.

D. Only if Steve provides over half of his child's overall support, and also obtains a signed **Form 8332,** *Release/Revocation of Release of Claim to Exemption for Child by Custodial Parent.*

37. Jamal received $1,600 in interest income in 2011. How should this income be reported on Jamal's tax return?

A. On page one of Form 1040.

B. On Schedule B.

C. On Schedule D.

D. On Form 1099-DIV.

38. Janice is the sole proprietor of a restaurant that had a net profit of $25,000 in 2011. Her husband, Marty, is also self-employed. Marty runs a carpentry business that had a net loss of $1,500 in 2011. Janice and Marty file jointly. How should this income and loss be reported?

A. Janice and Marty may file a single Schedule C netting the income and loss from both businesses. The Schedule SE will show total earnings subject to SE tax of $23,500.

B. Janice must file a Schedule C for the restaurant showing her net profit of $25,000 and Marty must file his own Schedule C for the carpentry business showing his net loss of $1,500. Their Schedule SE will show total earnings subject to SE tax of $23,500.

C. Janice must file a Schedule C for the restaurant showing her net profit of $25,000 and Marty must file his own Schedule C for the carpentry business showing his net loss of $1,500. Janice's Schedule SE will show total earnings subject to SE tax of $25,000.

D. Janice must file a Schedule C for the restaurant showing her net profit of $25,000 and Marty must file his own Schedule C for the carpentry business showing his net loss of $1,500. Janice's Schedule SE will show total earnings subject to SE tax of $25,000. Marty's Schedule SE will show a credit for $1,500 (the amount of his loss).

39. Felix and Samantha sold their home on May 7, 2011. Through April 30, 2011 they made home mortgage interest payments of $12,200. The settlement sheet for the sale of the home showed an additional $50 in interest for the six-day period in May up to, but not including, the date of sale. They also had a mortgage prepayment penalty of $2,000. In March, they also paid $120 in late payment fees to their mortgage lender, due to a missed payment. How much is their allowable mortgage interest deduction in 2011?

A. $12,200.

B. $12,250.

C. $12,370.

D. $14,370.

40. Victoria and Pete divorced five years ago. Under her divorce settlement, she must pay her ex-husband $15,000 a year, which she has paid in equal installments each month. She is also required to pay his ongoing medical expenses for a condition he acquired during their marriage. In 2011, Pete's medical expenses were $11,400. She paid $10,000 of the medical expenses directly to the hospital. The other $1,400 she gave directly to Pete after getting a copy of the doctor's bill. How much of these payments can be properly deducted by Victoria as alimony?

A. Victoria may claim $15,000 in alimony as an adjustment to income.

B. Victoria may claim $15,000 in alimony paid as an adjustment to income, and $10,000 as a medical expense on **Schedule A** of her own return.

C. Victoria may claim $26,400 in alimony paid as an adjustment to income on her individual **Form 1040.**

D. Victoria may claim $26,400 in alimony paid as an itemized deduction on **Schedule A.**

41. In 2011 Laverne pays her attorney $8,000 for handling her divorce. After the divorce is final, Laverne's ex-husband refuses to pay the alimony. So Laverne pays an additional fee of $4,500 for legal services to ensure the alimony is collected. How much of the legal fees are deductible on Laverne's individual tax return, and how should they be reported?

A. $0; none of the legal expenses are deductible.

B. Laverne can deduct $4,500, subject to the 2% limit, as a miscellaneous itemized deduction.

C. Laverne can deduct $4,500, NOT subject to the 2% limit, as a miscellaneous itemized deduction.

D. Laverne can deduct $12,500, subject to the 2% limit, as a miscellaneous itemized deduction.

42. Kayla, who is eight years old, has a small role in a television series. She made $65,000 during the tax year, but her parents put all the money in a trust fund to pay for college. Her parents have a joint AGI of $41,000. Kayla lived at home all year. Does she meet the support test in order for her parents to claim her as a dependent?

A. Yes, Kayla meets the support test, and her parents can claim her as a dependent.

B. No, Kayla does not meet the support test, and her parents cannot claim her as a dependent.

C. Since Kayla made the most money in the household, she can legally file her own tax return as "Single" and claim her parents as dependents.

D. None of the above.

43. Which of the following would prevent a taxpayer from being eligible for the Earned Income Tax Credit?

A. Being married to a resident alien with a valid Social Security Number.

B. Using the Head of Household filing status.

C. Correctly claiming the foreign earned income exclusion on Form 2555.

D. Filing a joint return with a spouse who died in 2011.

44. Patrick is 65, and he experiences age discrimination on the job. He decides to sue his company. After he files the lawsuit, he is attacked by the company owner, who breaks Patrick's arm when he pushes him. The court eventually awards Patrick the following amounts:

- $4,000 for emotional distress
- $10,000 for loss of wages
- $35,000 for physical injury related to the assault

How much of this award is taxable to Patrick as ordinary income?

A. $0.

B. $4,000.

C. $10,000.

D. $14,000.

E. $49,000.

45. In 2011, Sarah worked at Company A and earned $60,000 before she switched employers. At Company B, Sarah earns $50,000. Social Security taxes were withheld from the full amount of her wages, but the maximum earnings subject to Social Security tax for the year is only $106,800. Which of the following statements is TRUE?

A. Sarah cannot get an IRS refund of the overpaid Social Security. She must ask her employer to return the amount to her on her next paycheck.

B. Sarah can claim a refund of the Social Security taxes withheld from the last $3,200 in earnings when she files her 2011 personal income tax return.

C. Sarah can claim the Retirement Savings Contribution Credit and use the overpaid amounts as her credit.

D. Sarah can carry over the overpaid Social Security tax on $3,200 as a credit on future wages.

46. Gabrielle adopted a child whose adoption was final in 2011. Gabrielle had \$14,500 in out-of-pocket adoption expenses in 2011. Her tax liability for the year is \$3,500. What is her maximum allowable Adoption Credit in 2011?

A. \$0.

B. \$3,500.

C. \$13,360.

D. \$14,500.

47. Terry is Married Filing Separately. She has a dependent child in daycare. Terry has signed up for a Flexible Spending Account at work and has had \$2,500 taken out of her wages for daycare costs. She paid \$3,000 in daycare costs during the year. Which of the following statements is TRUE?

A. Terry can exclude the \$3,000 from her wages as part of the Flexible Spending Account.

B. Terry can exclude \$2,500 from income. She can take the Child and Dependent Care Credit for the remaining \$500.

C. Terry can exclude a total of \$2,500 from her gross income. She may not claim the Child and Dependent Care Credit for the remaining \$500.

D. Terry cannot exclude any amount because she is Married Filing Separately. All the benefits are therefore taxable to Terry as ordinary income.

48. Matt is an investor. He subscribes to *Forbes* and *Kiplinger* magazines. Matt also pays for a safe deposit box where he holds his investments and stock certificates. Which of the following statements is the best answer?

A. Matt may deduct these expenses on **Schedule A** as a miscellaneous itemized deduction subject to the 2% floor.

B. Matt may deduct these expenses on **Schedule A** as a miscellaneous itemized deduction NOT subject to the 2% floor.

C. Matt may NOT deduct these expenses.

D. Matt may deduct these expenses on **Schedule C** as a business expense.

49. Leigh is single, 58, and works for XYZ Corporation. She has a traditional IRA retirement plan with XYZ Corporation that is currently valued at $79,000. On December 1, 2011 Leigh dies. Her only son Tom, age 27, inherits the retirement plan. Which of the following statements is true?

A. Tom must start taking minimum distributions from the retirement plan, which will be subject to the 10% early withdrawal penalty, since Tom is not 59½.

B. Tom may roll over the inherited retirement plan into his own retirement plan, essentially treating it as his own.

C. Tom may choose to take a lump sum distribution or start taking minimum distributions from the retirement plan, which will NOT be subject to the 10% early withdrawal penalty. He cannot roll over the inherited retirement plan into his own existing plan.

D. Tom cannot start taking distributions from his inherited retirement plan until he reaches 59½.

50. Benny and Donna Smith are investors in a mutual fund. In 2011, the mutual fund notified the Smiths that they had $12,000 in capital gains. However, only $5,000 was actually distributed to the Smiths in 2011. What is the correct amount of capital gain that the Smiths must report on their 2011 tax return?

A. $0.

B. $5,000.

C. $7,000.

D. $12,000.

51. Ellen started her own catering business in 2011. She paid $10,000 for a delivery van, contributed $20,000 of her own savings in cash to the business, and also purchased $13,000 in equipment, glassware, and other tools on her personal credit cards. What is her at-risk amount for this business activity?

A. $0.

B. $10,000.

C. $30,000.

D. $43,000.

52. Pam owns a 50% interest in a residential rental house. Last year she paid $968 to repair a broken window. She replaced it with a premium energy-saving window. What is the correct treatment of this expense?

A. Pam cannot deduct the cost since it was an improvement (an upgrade); she must add it to the basis of the property.

B. Pam can deduct $484 (50% × $968) as a rental expense on **Schedule E.** She is entitled to reimbursement for the remaining half from the co-owner.

C. Pam can deduct $968 as a rental expense on **Schedule E.**

D. Pam can deduct $968 on **Schedule A** as an itemized deduction.

53. Ursula is unmarried and has two qualifying children. They are both full-time students. Lila is 21 and a junior in college. Lila had $5,000 in tuition expenses in 2011. Lynette is 23 and attends graduate school for her master's degree. Lynette had $6,000 in tuition expenses in 2011. Assuming that Ursula meets all the other requirements for claiming the credit, what is the maximum American Opportunity Credit that Ursula can take on her 2011 tax return?

A. Ursula may take $2,500 as an American Opportunity Credit for Lila only.

B. Ursula may take $2,500 as an American Opportunity Credit for Lila, and another $2,500 for Lynette.

C. Ursula may claim a total of $8,000 ($4,000 for each student) as an American Opportunity Credit.

D. Ursula may take $4,000 as an American Opportunity Credit for Lila only.

54. Clark received a scholarship to attend San Francisco State University. He decides to take three classes, but he is not a degree candidate. The scholarship is for $5,000. Clark's tuition was $3,000 and his books were $900. He had no other education expenses. How much of the scholarship is taxable to Clark?

A. $0.

B. $2,000.

C. $1,100.

D. $5,000.

55. David moved to a new home 40 miles from his former home because he changed job locations. His old job was three miles from his former home. His new job location is 60 miles from that home. David paid $3,000 to move his belongings to his new home. He also paid $150 in storage fees during the move and had $50 in meal expenses while moving. Which of the following statements is TRUE?

A. David's moving expenses are not deductible because he does not meet the distance test.

B. David may deduct all his moving expenses ($3,000 + $150) EXCEPT for the cost of his meals ($50).

C. David may deduct only the $3,000 in actual moving expenses. The cost of the meals and storage fees are not deductible.

D. David may deduct all the costs related to his move, including the cost of meals.

56. In order to meet the "substantial presence" test in determining residency for IRS purposes, an individual must be physically present in the United States for at least ______ days over a three-year period.

A. 214.

B. 183.

C. 120.

D. 365.

57. Ramon is a U.S. citizen serving in the Navy in Japan. His wife and children live with him, and he is able to claim the children as dependents. Ramon's wife, a citizen of Japan, chooses not to be treated as a resident alien for tax purposes. She does not want to file a joint return with him. Which of the following statements is TRUE?

A. Ramon may not file a return until he comes back to the United States.

B. Ramon may file as Head of Household and claim his children as dependents.

C. Since Ramon is married and living with his spouse, he cannot claim Head of Household status. He must file Married Filing Separately.

D. Ramon may still file jointly with his wife and sign on her behalf, since his wife is a non-resident alien.

58. Carol and Javier are married and plan to file a joint return. Carol is 66 and had gross income of $11,000 for the tax year. Javier is also 66. His gross income was $5,000 for the year. They have no dependents. Which of the following is the best answer?

A. They are required to file a tax return.

B. They do not have to file a return.

C. Carol is required to file a tax return.

D. They should file a tax return, because they qualify for the Earned Income Credit.

59. Which of the following individuals must file a tax return?

A. Rose, 68, who is widowed and supported by her son. She had $8,000 in Social Security income for 2011.

B. Frances, 70, whose only source of income in 2011 was her pension of $10,600.

C. Emmett, 64, a single taxpayer with $2,000 in self-employment income and $4,500 in Social Security income.

D. None of the above must file a tax return.

60. Who of the following is required to have an Individual Taxpayer Identification Number (ITIN)?

A. All non-resident aliens.

B. All non-resident and resident aliens.

C. Anyone who doesn't have a Social Security Number.

D. All non-resident and resident aliens who must file a return or who are claimed on someone else's return and are not eligible for a valid SSN.

61. Generally, how long should taxpayers keep the supporting documentation for their tax returns?

A. Four years from the due date.

B. Three years from the due date.

C. Two years from the due date.

D. At least one year after the due date.

62. Two years ago, Alice paid $1,050 for 100 shares of ABC, Inc. stock, plus a broker's commission of $50. Alice received ten additional shares of ABC stock as a non-taxable stock dividend. What is the current adjusted basis of Alice's stock?

A. $9 per share.

B. $10 per share.

C. $11 per share.

D. $25 per share.

63. Eric and Zelda are married but will not file a joint return together. Both are 40 years old. Eric's gross income from wages is $30,150, and Zelda's wage income is $3,700. Which of the following is true?

A. Only Eric is required to file.

B. Only Zelda is required to file.

C. Both Eric and Zelda are required to file.

D. Neither Eric nor Zelda must file.

64. Three years ago, Lenny bought 500 shares of XYZ Corporation stock for $1,500, including his broker's commission. On April 6, 2011, XYZ distributed a 2% non-taxable stock dividend (10 shares). Three months later, on July 6, 2011, Lenny sold all 510 shares of his XYZ stock for $2,030. What is the nature of Lenny's gain?

A. Lenny has a long-term capital gain.

B. Lenny has a short-term capital gain.

C. Lenny has an ordinary gain.

D. Lenny must prorate his gain between the short-term gains and long-term gains. Five hundred shares will have long-term capital gain treatment, and the remainder will have short-term capital gain treatment.

65. Nora has one **Form W-2** for $22,000 and one **Form 1099-INT** and no other income. Her **Form 1099-INT** shows both interest income of $2,000 and an early withdrawal penalty of $450. Nora will not itemize deductions, and she cannot claim any tax credits. Which of the following statements is TRUE?

A. Since Nora does not itemize, she cannot deduct the early withdrawal penalty of $450.

B. Nora can claim an adjustment for the penalty on early withdrawal of savings on **Form 1040.**

C. Nora can claim the adjustment for the penalty on early withdrawal on **Form 1040-EZ**.

D. Nora is precluded from claiming the penalty for early withdrawal this year, but the amount can be treated as a carryover to a future year to offset investment income.

66. Mark and Carmen are divorced. Their daughter, Stephanie, lives with Carmen, who claims her as a dependent. Carmen paid for and deducted Stephanie's medical and dental bills. Mark also paid a $5,000 emergency medical bill when Stephanie broke her arm. Carmen will not release their child's dependency exemption to Mark. Regarding the medical expense that Mark paid for his child, which of the following is correct?

A. Only a custodial parent can claim a deduction for a child's medical expenses.

B. Only the parent who claims the dependency exemption can claim medical expenses paid on behalf of the child.

C. Mark may deduct the emergency bill he paid, even if he does not claim Stephanie as his dependent.

D. None of the above is correct.

67. Harvey, 73, and Candy, 66, are married and live together. They both work and each has a traditional IRA. In 2011, Harvey earned $2,000 in wages, and Candy earned $30,000. If they file separate returns, what is the maximum that Harvey can contribute to his IRA?

A. $0.

B. $2,000.

C. $5,000.

D. $6,000.

68. All of the following are deductible medical expenses EXCEPT ______.

A. Acupuncture.

B. Transportation to a medical conference related to the chronic disease of a dependent.

C. Birth control pills.

D. Non-prescription nicotine gum and patches.

69. Which form is used by a college to report tuition and fees paid by a taxpayer during the year?

A. Form 1099-T.

B. Form 1098-T.

C. Form 1098.

D. Form 1099-B.

70. Olga paid the following taxes and fees in 2011: state income tax, $2,000; real estate taxes, $1,900; DMV fees, $100; homeowners' association fee, $250. What is Olga's total deduction for taxes on **Schedule A**?

A. $1,900.

B. $3,900.

C. $4,000.

D. $4,150.

71. Two years ago, Keith and Tiffany obtained home equity loans totaling $91,000. The couple used the loans to pay off gambling debts, overdue credit payments, and some other expenses. The current balance of their home equity loan is $72,000. The fair market value of their home is $230,000, and they carry $30,000 of outstanding acquisition debt on the home. If Keith and Tiffany file jointly, can they deduct the interest they pay on these loans?

A. Yes, they can deduct the interest on their loans.

B. No, they cannot deduct the interest on their loans.

C. The interest on the loans is only partially deductible and must be prorated to the amount of acquisition debt on their home.

D. None of the above.

72. Hana has contributed to a Roth IRA for the last four years. This year, she took the full amount of her Roth IRA as a distribution to help her purchase her first home. Which of the following statements regarding this distribution is correct?

A. The entire distribution is excluded from her taxable income.

B. Only the return of her regular contributions is not included in her gross income. Any earnings are taxable.

C. The entire distribution is taxable.

D. The entire distribution is taxable, and is also subject to a 10% early withdrawal penalty.

73. Which of the following is a qualified charitable deduction?

A. The cost of a raffle ticket at a church fundraiser.

B. Blood donated to the Red Cross.

C. Out-of-pocket travel expenses for a volunteer to attend a church fundraiser.

D. Direct contributions to a homeless individual.

74. Sonny is a general partner in the LMN Partnership. How should Sonny report his distributive share of partnership income on his individual tax return?

A. Sonny's partnership income should be reported on Schedule C, Form 1040.

B. Sonny's share of partnership income should be reported on Schedule E, Form 1040.

C. Sonny's share of partnership income should be reported on Schedule F, Form 1040.

D. Sonny's share of partnership income should be reported on Schedule L, Form 1040.

75. Paloma bought her home two years ago. She started having difficulty making their mortgage payments. In 2011, Paloma's mortgage lender agreed to reduce the principal on her home loan and refinance it with a better interest rate and lower monthly payments. The principal balance before the refinance was $230,000, and the lender reduced the principal loan amount to $200,000. The home has never been used for business or as rental property, and Paloma has not filed for bankruptcy. She continued to live in the home as her primary residence. Based on this information, how should Paloma report this transaction?

A. Report the transaction as non-taxable canceled debt on **Form 982**.

B. Report the transaction as a reduction in the basis of the home on line 10b of **Form 982**.

C. Report the $30,000 as a loss on **Schedule D**.

D. Include $30,000 of debt cancellation in taxable income on **Form 1040**.

76. Mai Lin is single. In 2011, she has $120,000 in wage income. She also owns a residential rental property that has a $28,000 loss for the year. Mai Lin actively participated in the rental activity. How much of her rental loss is deductible in the current year?

A. $0.

B. $15,000.

C. $25,000.

D. $28,000.

77. Which of the following taxpayers qualifies for the First Time Homebuyer Credit in 2011?

A. A homebuyer who was on official extended duty as a member of the uniformed services.

B. A homebuyer who is a non-resident alien.

C. A homebuyer who disposes of the residence before the close of a taxable year.

D. None of the above; the First Time Homebuyer Credit expired in 2010.

78. Raymond has a traditional IRA. Rollover rules allow Raymond to do which one of the following WITHOUT incurring any income tax or penalty?

A. Roll over funds from his traditional IRA plan to a Roth IRA account.

B. Roll over his traditional IRA into the IRA of a spouse.

C. Roll over funds into a government deferred-compensation plan.

D. Rollover into an educational savings plan.

79. Mike's cost basis was $2,400 for 900 shares of Deva Corporation stock he purchased in June 2004. Mike sold the 900 shares on December 12, 2011 for $4,400 and paid an additional $100 commission. The gross proceeds from the sale were $4,400 on **Form 1099-B.** What was the sales price for the shares and the amount of capital gain?

A. $4,400 sales price and $2,000 gain.

B. $4,400 sales price and $1,900 gain.

C. $4,500 sales price and $2,100 gain.

D. $4,300 sales price and $1,900 gain.

80. Carlos moves to another city in 2011, and he decides to convert his former home into a residential rental property. Three years ago, Carlos bought his home for $182,000. At the time of the purchase, the value of the land was assessed at $20,000. On the date of the conversion, Carlos's property had a fair market value of $168,000, of which $21,000 was for the land and $147,000 was for the house. What is Carlos's basis of depreciation for the rental property?

A. $134,000.

B. $147,000.

C. $162,000.

D. $182,000.

81. Kyle sold all his shares in a mutual fund. The sale resulted in a capital loss of $7,000. Kyle has wages of $32,000 in 2011. He has no other income or losses. What is Kyle's adjusted gross income in 2011?

A. $25,000.

B. $29,000.

C. $32,000.

D. Some other amount.

82. Kevin is a member of the U.S. Army who has been serving in a combat zone since March 1. Is Kevin entitled to an extension of time for filing and paying his federal income taxes, and will penalties and interest be assessed on Kevin's delinquent tax return?

A. Kevin is granted an extension on his filing deadline, and he will not be charged interest or penalties attributable to the extension period.

B. Kevin is granted an extension on his filing deadline, but he will be charged interest attributable to the extension period.

C. Kevin is not granted an extension on his filing deadline, but he will not be charged interest or penalties attributable to the extension period.

D. Kevin is not granted an extension on his filing deadline.

83. In 2011, Elizabeth gave the following gifts:

- $13,000 to her sister Marjorie
- $16,000 for her grandson Timothy's tuition, which was paid directly to the college
- $14,000 to her uncle Frank
- $15,000 to the Democratic Party

How should these gifts be reported under the gift tax rules?

A. Marjorie and Frank are required to file gift tax returns and pay tax on the gifts.

B. Elizabeth must file a gift tax return only for the $14,000 gift to Frank.

C. Elizabeth must file a gift tax return for the gifts to Frank and Timothy.

D. All of the gifts are reportable.

84. Josh, a full-time student with no compensation, marries Larissa during the year. Both are age 27. For the year, Larissa has taxable compensation of $50,000. She plans to contribute the maximum to her traditional IRA. If Josh and Larissa file jointly, how much can each contribute to a traditional IRA?

A. Larissa can contribute $5,000 to her traditional IRA.

B. Larissa can contribute $5,000 to her traditional IRA, and also make a spousal contribution of $5,000 for Josh to his traditional IRA.

C. Larissa and Josh can both contribute $6,000 to a traditional IRA.

D. None of the above.

85. All of the following are deductible moving expenses in 2011, except:

A. The cost of moving pets.

B. Lodging during the move.

C. The cost of meals while moving.

D. The cost of packing materials.

86. In 2011, the maximum amount taxpayers may claim for the non-refundable Child Tax Credit is ______ for each qualifying child.

A. $500.

B. $1,000.

C. $3,700.

D. Some other amount.

87. A fire destroyed Chelsea's home. The home had an adjusted basis of $80,000 and the insurance company paid Chelsea $130,000 for the loss. Chelsea bought a replacement home for $100,000. How much is her gain (if any), and her basis in her new home?

A. Chelsea does not have a taxable gain. Her basis in the new home is $130,000.

B. Chelsea has a taxable gain of $30,000. Her basis in the new home is $80,000.

C. Chelsea has a taxable gain of $50,000. Her basis in the new home is $80,000.

D. Chelsea has a taxable gain of $30,000. Her basis in the new home is $100,000.

88. Chuck purchased his main home five years ago. He sells his home in June 2011. Chuck marries Jayme in September 2011. For the purpose of the Section 121 exclusion, Chuck meets the ownership and use tests, but Jayme does not. On their jointly filed return, how would Chuck report the sale of his home?

A. Chuck cannot exclude any of the gain from the sale of his home, because Jayme does not meet the ownership and use tests.

B. Chuck and Jayme can exclude up to $500,000 of gain on a joint return for 2011.

C. Chuck can exclude up to $250,000 of gain on their joint return for 2011.

D. None of the above.

89. Kris owns a vacation home by the lake. In 2011, Kris rented the home for two weeks, earning $1,200. She also lived in the home for four months. Kris paid $5,000 in mortgage interest on the home in 2011. The remainder of the year the home was vacant. What is the proper treatment of this activity?

A. Kris does not have to report the rental income. The mortgage interest is deductible on Schedule A as an itemized deduction.

B. The rental income should be reported on Schedule E, and the mortgage interest is deductible on Schedule A as an itemized deduction.

C. The rental income and mortgage interest should be reported on Schedule E.

D. The rental income can be reported as "other income" on Form 1040. The mortgage interest is not deductible, since it is a vacation home.

90. Wilson owns a two bedroom apartment which he rents. He is a self-employed Enrolled Agent and works exclusively out of a home office. In 2011, Wilson paid $1,000 a month in rent for his apartment. He also paid $50 a month in utilities. His home office is 240 square feet (12 feet × 20 feet). The total square footage of his apartment is 1,200 square feet. Ignoring any income limitations, what is Wilson's allowable deduction for home office expense?

A. $1,050.

B. $1,200.

C. $2,520.

D. $12,600.

91. Angel is a nurse working for Mercy General Hospital. Angel attended a continuing education course in Los Angeles. His expenses related to the trip were as follows:

- Lodging: $300
- Airfare to the event: $245
- Meals: $60
- Fees for the course: $150

What is Angel's deductible educational expense?

A. $150.

B. $395.

C. $725.

D. $755.

92. Scott is a police officer. In 2011, he pays $450 for new uniforms and $300 for dry cleaning the uniforms. How much of this expense is deductible, and how would the expense be reported?

A. $0; the costs are not deductible.

B. $450 (the cost of the uniforms) is deductible as a miscellaneous itemized deduction, subject to the 2% floor.

C. $750 is deductible as a miscellaneous itemized deduction, NOT subject to the 2% floor.

D. $750 is deductible as a miscellaneous itemized deduction, subject to the 2% floor.

93. Jean owns a business office. She allows her church to use the building rent-free for six months. Jean normally rents the office for $600. However, other offices are renting for $700 in the same building, so the fair market value of the rental is $700 per month. How much can Jean deduct as a charitable deduction?

A. $0.

B. $3,600.

C. $4,200.

D. $7,200.

94. In 2011, Audrey discovers that her housekeeper stole personal property from her. The property had an adjusted basis of $4,000 and a fair market value of $10,000. Audrey's adjusted gross income in 2011 is $24,000. What is Audrey's casualty loss deduction (after applying the $100 and 10% limitations)?

A. $1,500.

B. $2,400.

C. $7,500.

D. $8,910.

95. In 2011, Liam installs $20,000 in qualifying energy-efficient exterior windows on his main home. What is the maximum amount of his Residential Energy Property Credit?

A. $200.

B. $1,500.

C. $5,000.

D. $20,000.

96. Which of the following statements regarding Roth retirement plans is FALSE?

A. A Roth IRA requires minimum distributions at age 70½.

B. A Roth IRA does not permit a tax deduction at the time of contribution.

C. Married taxpayers who file separate returns (MFS) may contribute to a Roth IRA.

D. "Compensation" for the purpose of a Roth IRA does not include earnings and profits from rental property.

97. Gregory and Flavia are married, but file separate tax returns. In 2011, Gregory sells 300 shares of ABC Company stock. The stock value had fallen, and he has a $4,000 long-term capital loss on the sale. He has no other capital gains or losses. Within 15 days after Gregory sells his stock, Flavia purchases 500 shares of stock in the same company (ABC Company). How should the stock sale be reported on Gregory's separate tax return?

A. Gregory may deduct the $4,000 on his tax return as a long-term capital loss.

B. Gregory may deduct $3,000 of the loss on his tax return, and the remaining $1,000 must be carried over to the next year.

C. Gregory can deduct the loss only if he files jointly with Flavia. Otherwise, the entire loss is treated as a carryover.

D. Gregory has a wash sale, and he may not deduct the loss.

98. Pastor Green is a full-time minister. The church allows him to use a parsonage that has an annual fair rental value of $24,000. The church also pays Pastor Green an annual salary of $67,000, of which $7,500 is designated for his home utility costs. Pastor Green's actual utility costs during the year were $7,000. What is Pastor Green's income for self-employment tax purposes?

A. $500.

B. $60,000.

C. $67,000.

D. $91,000.

99. Theo agrees to sell his vacation property to a buyer under an installment sale. He sells the property at a contract price of $120,000, and his gross profit is $15,000. Theo will receive four equal payments (one payment per year) until the note is paid off. Theo receives the first payment of $30,000 in 2011. The first payment does not include any interest. He wants to use the installment method to report income from the sale. What is the amount of installment sale income that Theo will report in 2011?

A. $0.

B. $3,750.

C. $7,500.

D. $15,000.

100. Jasmine is a self-employed Enrolled Agent, and she files a Schedule C. In which of the following instances would Jasmine NOT be required to obtain an Employer Identification Number (EIN)?

A. When she hires an employee.

B. When she forms a partnership with her husband.

C. When she operates multiple sole proprietorships.

D. When she files bankruptcy under Chapter 7.

Please review your answers with the answers in the back.

# Part 2: Businesses Practice Exam

1. Davenport Inc. is a fiscal year C Corporation that reports income and loss on the accrual basis. Which of the following is required for Davenport to accrue and deduct an expense?

A. Davenport Inc. must first pay the expense in order to accrue and deduct it.

B. Davenport Inc. must first receive an invoice or other bill in order to accrue and deduct it.

C. Davenport Inc. must meet the all events test and have economic performance in order to deduct the expense.

D. Davenport Inc. must have received a bill for the expense and paid it before the end of its fiscal year.

2. What is the accumulated earnings tax?

A. A 15% tax that is assessed on S Corporation and partnership profits.

B. A 15% tax that is assessed on the accumulated earnings and profits of a C Corporation.

C. A 20% tax that is imposed upon estates.

D. A 15% payroll tax that is imposed in addition to the Trust Fund Recovery penalty.

3. Terries Corporation offers fringe benefits to its employees. Which of the following benefits is taxable to the employee?

A. Health insurance provided to an employee by the employer.

B. The value of $100,000 in life insurance coverage provided to an employee.

C. Employer-provided parking passes.

D. Employee discounts on merchandise.

4. The Darby Corporation was organized on May 15. It elected the calendar year as its accounting period. When is the tax return due for this corporation?

A. October 15.

B. April 15.

C. March 15.

D. May 31.

5. Most entities may choose whether to be taxed as a partnership or a corporation. Which of the following answers is FALSE regarding the formation of a business entity?

A. Any eligible entity with two or more members may be classified as a partnership.

B. Any domestic LLC with a single member is disregarded as an entity by the IRS. Any income or losses are then taxable to the owner, just like a sole proprietorship.

C. Partnerships file Form 1065 to report income and losses.

D. A non-profit entity that is classified as a corporation must file Form 1120 for tax purposes.

6. Rick wants to transfer assets to a corporation in exchange for a controlling interest in the corporation's stock. Which of the following transfers would create a TAXABLE event under IRC Sec. 351 for Rick?

A. Rick exchanged property in exchange for 100% of the corporation's stock.

B. The corporation assumes liabilities in excess of the basis of the assets transferred.

C. Cash is exchanged for 100% of the corporate stock.

D. Rick will not be required to recognize any gain in a transfer, so long as he has a controlling interest (over 80%) in the corporation's stock after the transfer.

7. All of the following entities are required to use the accrual method of accounting, EXCEPT:

A. A family farming corporation with gross receipts of $24 million.

B. A C Corporation with gross receipts of $50 million.

C. A tax shelter with $30,000 in gross receipts.

D. A corporation with $50,000 in gross income and long-term contracts.

8. Paul and his sister, Susan, have formed a Limited Liability Company (LLC). If they do not file Form 8832, *Entity Classification Election*, how will the IRS classify their business entity?

A. As a qualified family joint venture, with two separate sole proprietorships.

B. As a partnership.

C. As a C Corporation.

D. As an S Corporation.

9. In 2011, the Morrison Corporation purchases a number of assets, which all qualify for Section 179 treatment:

- Equipment: $100,000
- New computer: $5,000
- Qualified leasehold improvements: $350,000

The Morrison Corporation is not subject to any income limitations. What is their maximum *allowable* Section 179 deduction in 2011?

A. $105,000.

B. $250,000.

C. $355,000.

D. $455,000.

10. Music Web Corporation is a domestic corporation that runs a website selling digital music. One overseas band, the Australian Rock Stars, wants to use the web service to host and sell their music downloads. This Australian band does not have an EIN, ITIN, or SSN. In this scenario, which of the following statements is TRUE?

A. Music Web cannot do business with the Australian Rock Stars because they do not have a Taxpayer Identification Number.

B. Music Web is required to withhold tax at a flat rate of 28%.

C. Music Web is required to withhold tax at a flat rate of 30%.

D. Music Web is not required to withhold tax because the band lives overseas.

11. Sunway Partnership is a calendar-year, cash-basis entity. In 2011, Sunway provided services to a client and, in exchange, the partnership received a used car with a fair market value of $8,000 and an adjusted basis of $7,500. The partnership also received design services with a value of $3,000. How much of this must the Sunway Partnership report as income in 2011?

A. $3,000.

B. $8,500.

C. $10,500.

D. $11,000.

12. Jessie and Trevor are general partners in the Midway Partnership. In 2011, they drove the company van 7,000 business-related miles out of a total of 10,000 miles, and had $5,500 in total gasoline expense. They also had to pay $25 for the annual state license tags, $20 for their city registration sticker, and $235 in DMV fees. They are claiming actual car expenses, rather than the standard mileage rate. What is their allowable business deduction for automobile expenses?

A. $3,500.

B. $4,046.

C. $5,780.

D. $8,137.

13. Gulls Corp. is a calendar-year corporation that completely dissolved on July 22, 2011. When is Gulls' final tax return due?

A. October 15, 2011.

B. April 15, 2012.

C. March 15, 2011.

D. October 15, 2012.

14. Which of the following taxes is NOT applicable to a partnership?

A. Employment taxes.

B. Excise taxes.

C. Penalties for late filing.

D. Self-employment tax.

15. Which of the following entities is NOT required to e-file their business return?

A. A partnership with 200 partners (Schedules K-1).

B. A corporation with assets of $10 million or more that files at least 250 returns annually.

C. A sole proprietorship with 100 employees.

D. A small tax-exempt organization that wishes to file Form 990-N.

16. Which of the following non-profit entities is required to file an annual information return?

A. A private foundation with income of $5,000.

B. A church.

C. A government entity.

D. An organization that is a subordinate of a parent organization.

17. Doomsday Inc. is a calendar-year corporation that pays $3,000 in 2011 for a business insurance policy that is effective for three years, beginning on July 1, 2011. How much of the insurance policy is deductible on Doomsday's 2011 tax return?

A. $250.

B. $500.

C. $1,750.

D. $3,000.

18. Which IRS form is used by a sole proprietor to calculate and report the business-use of a home office?

A. Form 8829.

B. Form 2106.

C. Schedule A.

D. Form 8889.

19. Which of the following would NOT be excludable from an employee's wages as a *de minimis* fringe benefit?

A. Group-term life insurance payable on the death of an employee's spouse with a face value amount of $2,000.

B. Occasional picnics or parties for employees.

C. Transportation fare.

D. A $100 gift card as a holiday gift.

20. Carson Corporation sets up an IRA for its employees. The IRA is a payroll-deduction retirement account, where the amounts are taken from an employee's wages and deposited directly into each employee's individual IRA. Regarding this type of employer retirement arrangement, which of the following is FALSE?

A. Participants are always 100% vested in all of the funds in their IRAs.

B. Participant loans are permitted.

C. IRA withdrawals are permitted any time.

D. An employee may move the IRA assets from one IRA provider to another.

21. Janelle owns a bookstore. She recently signed a contract with a vendor, which was finalized over dinner. The total cost of the dinner was $250. Janelle's own dinner was $50. The vendor ate an expensive meal and also drank liquor, so his portion of the meal was $170. The remainder of the bill was for the tip and tax. Janelle also spent $10 in taxi fare to get to the meal. How much of this expense is actually deductible by Janelle as a business expense?

A. $25.

B. $110.

C. $135.

D. $250.

22. Manny is an attorney. He transfers property worth $150,000 and renders legal services valued at $13,000 to the Beltway Corporation in exchange for stock valued at $138,000. Right after the exchange, Manny owns 85% of the outstanding corporate stock. How much gain or loss does Manny recognize in this transaction?

A. $1,000 in capital loss.

B. $13,000 in ordinary income.

C. $12,000 in capital loss and $13,000 in ordinary income.

D. No gain or loss is recognized in this transaction.

23. Alex sold his office building to Cheryl, a real estate investor, who plans to use it as a business rental property. Alex was liable for $2,000 in delinquent real estate taxes on the property, which Cheryl agreed to pay. Which of the following statements is TRUE?

A. Cheryl can deduct these taxes as a business expense.

B. Cheryl cannot deduct these taxes as a current expense, but should instead add the amount to her basis of the property.

C. Alex can deduct these taxes as an expense because he was the legal owner of the property.

D. The expense must be divided equally between Alex and Cheryl in order to be deductible.

24. Harrington Corporation does a Section 1031 exchange with an airplane (adjusted basis $30,000) for another airplane (FMV $75,000). Harrington also pays an additional $40,000 in cash to complete the exchange. What is Harrington's basis in the new plane?

A. $70,000.

B. $75,000.

C. $105,000.

D. $115,000.

25. A calendar-year C Corporation would like to change to a fiscal year end. How can the corporation change its tax year?

A. A C corporation may file a short period return and elect a fiscal year at any time during its existence without IRS consent.

B. The C Corporation may switch to a fiscal year so long as it has not changed its annual accounting period at any time within the last 12 months.

C. The C Corporation may request a change in its tax year by filing Form 1128.

D. The C Corporation must dissolve before changing its accounting period.

26. Which of the following is NOT included in the Cost of Goods Sold inventory calculation?

A. The cost of products or raw materials, including freight.

B. Storage costs for finished products.

C. Contributions to pension or annuity plans for workers who produce the products.

D. The cost of shipping finished products to customers.

27. U.S. tax law requires businesses to submit a Form 1099 for every contractor paid at least _______________ for services during a year.

A. $400.

B. $600.

C. $850.

D. $1,000.

28. Mario and Juan decide to form an equal partnership. Mario contributes $30,000, and Juan contributes property with an FMV of $40,000 and an adjusted basis of $25,000. What is the basis of each partner?

A. Mario has a $30,000 basis, and Juan has a $25,000 basis.

B. Mario has a $30,000 basis, and Juan has a $40,000 basis.

C. Mario has a $25,000 basis, and Juan has a $25,000 basis.

D. None of the above.

29. Which of the following would NOT be allowed to be an S Corporation shareholder?

A. An estate.

B. A non-resident alien.

C. A U.S. resident who is not an American citizen.

D. A 501(c)(3) corporation.

30. Which of the following would be classified as a "guaranteed payment" to a partner in a partnership?

A. A partner only receives the payment if the partnership earns a profit.

B. A payment that was contractually obligated, but remained unpaid at the end of the partnership's taxable year.

C. A payment that a partner constructively received during the partnership's taxable year.

D. Answer B and C are correct.

31. Karen acquires a 20% interest in a partnership by contributing a building that had an adjusted basis to her of $800,000 and is encumbered by a $400,000 mortgage. The partnership assumes payment of the mortgage. The basis of Karen's partnership interest is:

A. $400,000.

B. $480,000.

C. $640,000.

D. $800,000.

32. The Kendall Corporation is a calendar-year C Corporation. Kendall Corp. has net income of $600,000 before its charitable contribution of $65,000. Kendall Corp. also has a net operating loss carryover of $200,000 from the prior year. What is Kendall's allowable charitable contribution in 2011?

A. $0.

B. $6,500.

C. $60,000.

D. $40,000.

33. Amino Corporation trades manufacturing equipment for new equipment in a qualified Section 1031 exchange. The cost of the old equipment was $50,000. The old equipment had $26,000 in accumulated depreciation. Amino also paid an additional $12,000 in cash to obtain the new equipment. What is Amino's adjusted basis in the new equipment after the exchange?

A. $24,000

B. $36,000

C. $50,000

D. $62,000

34. A qualified Personal Service Corporation is taxed at a flat rate of _____ on its taxable income.

A. 15%.

B. 30%.

C. 35%.

D. 45%.

35. Corporations generally must make estimated tax payments if they expect their estimated tax to be _____ or more.

A. $100.

B. $500.

C. $1,000.

D. $5,000.

36. ABC Corporation owns 85% of the outstanding stock in DDD Corporation. In 2011, ABC Corporation receives $250,000 in dividends from DDD Corporation. What percentage of the dividends does ABC Corporation have to pay taxes on?

A. 0%.

B. 10%.

C. 20%.

D. 30%.

37. Which of the following vehicles is NOT an "excepted vehicle" for the purpose of the listed property rules?

A. An ambulance.

B. A hearse.

C. A taxi.

D. All of the above are excepted vehicles.

38. Which of the following property is eligible for the Section 179 deduction?

A. Inventory.

B. Section 197 intangibles.

C. A patent.

D. Livestock.

39. Which of the following statements about a corporate stock distribution is CORRECT?

A. Stock distributions must be treated as a property distribution that is taxable to the shareholder.

B. Stock distributions are taxable to the corporation when distributed to shareholders.

C. Stock distributions are deductible by the corporation as an expense.

D. Stock distributions are not taxable to shareholders and not deductible by the corporation.

40. Devon is the sole owner and shareholder in Mechanics Corporation, a cash-basis S Corporation. In 2011, Mechanics Corp. had the following activity:

- Gross income from operations: $50,000
- Tax exempt interest: $1,000
- Residential rental income: $5,000
- Charitable contributions: $2,000
- Deductible business expenses: $20,000

How much **ordinary income** will be reported by the S Corporation?

A. $28,000.

B. $30,000.

C. $35,000.

D. $55,000.

41. Which of the following items is not factored into the calculation for ordinary income of a partnership?

A. Cost of Goods Sold.

B. Partnership contributions to a partner's IRA account.

C. Partnership contributions to an employee's IRA account.

D. Section 179 deduction.

42. Which of the following is NOT a pass-through entity?

A. Sole proprietorship.

B. S Corporation.

C. C Corporation.

D. Partnership.

43. Ryan is a 10% shareholder in Golden Corporation with an outstanding $10,000 loan to the corporation. Ryan files for bankruptcy and defaults on the loan. Golden Corporation cancels Ryan's debt in 2011. How should this cancellation of debt be reported?

A. Treat the debt cancellation as a $10,000 taxable distribution to Ryan.

B. Treat the debt cancellation as a liquidation of stock.

C. Treat the debt cancellation as wages to Ryan.

D. Treat the debt cancellation as a $10,000 return of capital.

44. Gracie Corporation owes one of its vendors $250,000 for a delinquent invoice. The vendor threatens to sue to recover the debt. Gracie Corp. agrees to transfer a commercial building to the vendor in order to satisfy the debt. Gracie Corp. purchased the building seven years ago for $190,000. How must this transaction be reported?

A. Gracie Corp. must recognize a taxable gain of $60,000.

B. Gracie Corp. must recognize forgiven debt of $250,000.

C. Gracie Corp. must recognize a taxable gain of $250,000.

D. Gracie Corp. can recognize a loss of $60,000 on the sale of the commercial building.

45. Build Rite Inc. is a cash-basis C Corporation and also a Personal Service Corporation. The corporation's net income in 2011 is $68,000 before applying a net operating loss carryover of $22,000 from the previous year. What is Build Rite's corporate tax due in 2011?

A. $10,200.

B. $23,800.

C. $46,000.

D. $16,100.

46. In which of the following instances would Gabe be treated as having constructive ownership of MORE than 50% of the partnership?

Ownership Percentages

A. Gabe 20%; Gabe's son 20%; Gabe's brother 60%.

B. Gabe 25%; Gabe's wife 10%; Gabe's aunt 75%.

C. Gabe 45%; Gabe's cousin 51%; Gabe's son 4%.

D. Gabe 45%; Gabe's cousin 55%.

47. Underwater Corporation is having financial trouble and liquidates in 2011. In the course of liquidation, Underwater distributes $10,000 in cash and a machine with a fair market value of $12,000 and an adjusted basis of $8,000 to Gordon, a 10% shareholder. Gordon's basis in his stock is $17,000. How much gain will Gordon recognize in this transaction?

A. $2,000.

B. $5,000.

D. $3,000.

E. $18,000.

48. Quigley Corporation rents a legitimate office space from its only employee-shareholder. The fair rental value of the office space is $4,500 per month, but the corporation pays the shareholder $6,000 per month, and the corporation deducts the full amount as rent expense. Which of the following statements is TRUE?

A. The IRS may reclassify the excess $1,500 per month in rental payments as a constructive dividend, and the corporation would lose that amount as a deduction.

B. The IRS may reclassify the entire $4,500 per month in rental payments as a constructive dividend.

C. The IRS may reclassify the entire $6,000 per month in rental payments as a constructive dividend.

D. The IRS may reclassify the excess $1,500 per month in rental payments as a stock dividend.

49. Grassroots Corporation repurchased all of its outstanding bonds in 2011 for $580,000. The bonds were originally issued two years ago for a face value of $550,000. How should this transaction be reported by Grassroots?

A. Grassroots has a $30,000 capital loss.

B. Grassroots has a $30,000 interest expense.

C. No gain or loss is recognized on a repurchase of a corporation's own securities.

D. Grassroots has a $30,000 ordinary gain.

50. Can a husband and wife operate a business as a sole proprietorship or do they need to be a partnership? Which of the following statements is TRUE?

A. A husband and wife may operate as a sole proprietorship and file a single Schedule C for both taxpayers.

B. A married couple who jointly operate a business may choose for each spouse to be treated as a sole proprietor by electing to file as a "qualified joint venture."

C. A husband and wife may not operate a partnership together because of the related party transaction rules.

D. None of the above.

51. A few years ago, Star Corporation purchased land at a cost of $90,000. In 2011, the land is condemned by the federal government for development of a railway. Star Corp. receives a $160,000 condemnation award for the land. Within the same year, Star Corp. purchases replacement land for $80,000. How much gain (if any) should Star Corporation recognize on this transaction?

A. $10,000.

B. $20,000.

C. $70,000.

D. $160,000.

52. Wendy runs a sole proprietorship. She hires her own 15-year-old daughter, Kylie, to answer phones part-time and do filing and other office tasks. Wendy pays her daughter a reasonable wage of $5,000 for the year. Which of the following statements about the wages for Kylie is incorrect?

A. Kylie's wages are subject to the "kiddie tax."

B. Wages paid to a taxpayer's child are not deductible.

C. Kylie's wages are not subject to Social Security and Medicare taxes.

D. Kylie's wages are subject to income tax withholding.

53. Jaime is the single owner shareholder of XYZ Corporation, which is a calendar-year, accrual-basis C Corporation. On December 31, 2011, XYZ had accrued a $20,000 bonus for Jaime and $32,000 in wage expenses for other employees. The wages and the bonus were not actually paid until January 15, 2012. How much of the wage expense (if any) can XYZ deduct on its 2011 tax return?

A. $0.

B. $20,000.

C. $32,000.

D. $52,000.

54. Andrew owns and operates a restaurant. He has ten servers working for him. Which of the following is NOT a requirement for employers who have tipped employees?

A. Tips are considered taxable income and are subject to federal income taxes.

B. Tips that an employee receives from customers are subject to withholding.

C. The employer must collect income tax, employee Social Security tax, and employee Medicare tax on the employee's tips.

D. All of the above are correct.

55. Which form is used by a C Corporation to report income and losses?

A. Form 1120.

B. Form 1120-W.

C. Form 1065.

D. Form 8832.

56. Blair forms an LLC in 2011. She wants her business to be classified as a corporation for tax purposes. What form must Blair file in order to elect this treatment?

A. Form 4898.

B. Form 8832.

C. Form 7006.

D. Form 8821.

57. An interest in a partnership is treated as a __________ when it is sold.

A. Loss.

B. Capital asset.

C. Section 1231 asset.

C. Section 197 intangible asset.

58. The Brookshire Partnership is having financial difficulties in 2011. The partners decide to file for bankruptcy. In this case, the debt cancellation income and tax attribute reduction occurs where?

A. At the partnership level. Tax attribute reduction is reported on the partnership return and reduces the income of the partnership.

B. Each partner's share of debt cancellation income must be reported on the partner's individual return.

C. The debt cancellation is not reported on the partnership return or on the partner's individual return.

D. A partnership cannot legally declare bankruptcy; the partners must declare bankruptcy individually.

59. Big Dollar Corporation has a fiscal year-end of June 30, 2011. Big Dollar files an extension. What is Big Dollar's NEW due date?

A. Sept 15, 2011.

B. Oct 15, 2012.

C. March 15, 2012.

D. April 15, 2012.

60. The Lento Corporation is a cash-basis C Corporation. Lento has $190,000 in taxable income in 2011. It also has a $21,000 capital loss from the prior year and a net operating loss of $35,000 from a prior year. The corporation did not have any capital gains income. Assuming a corporate tax rate of 39% for all income, what is Lento's income tax liability for the year?

A. $74,100.

B. $52,260.

C. $60,450.

D. $65,910.

61. In 2011, Expo Corporation distributed a non-dividend distribution of $800 to its sole shareholder, Ned. Ned's stock basis before the distribution is $1,000. What is the effect of this transaction?

A. Ned must report a $1,000 capital gain.

B. Ned must report a $200 capital loss.

C. Ned must reduce his stock basis by $800.

D. Ned must report $800 in capital gain.

62. A tax exempt 501 (c)(3) corporation has $1,200 in unrelated business income in 2011. How should this income be reported?

A. The entity should report the unrelated business income on Form 1120.

B. The IRS will revoke the exempt status of the organization if it has business income.

C. The entity should report the unrelated business income on Form 990-T.

D. The entity should report the income on Form 990.

63. Renee is a general partner in Brown Partnership. Renee receives a parcel of land from the partnership that has a fair market value of $50,000 but a basis of $40,000. Her basis in her partnership interest is $32,000. How must Renee recognize this transaction?

A. Renee must reduce her partnership basis to zero, and her basis in the land is $32,000.

B. Renee must reduce her partnership basis to zero, and her basis in the land is $40,000.

C. Renee must recognize a capital gain of $8,000, and her basis in the land is $50,000.

D. Renee must recognize a capital gain of $10,000, and her basis in the land is $50,000.

64. Jack is a self-employed carpenter. He purchased the following equipment in 2011:

| Video recorder | $195 |
|---|---|
| Laptop | $450 |
| Digital camera | $123 |
| Desk chair | $53 |
| Cellular phone | $75 |
| Work tools | $178 |
| Tool belt | $95 |
| **Total** | **$1,169** |

Of the overall equipment purchases, how much is considered *listed property* for depreciation purposes?

A. $0.

B. $768.

C. $843.

D. $1,041.

65. Conrad Corporation is a new company that elects to amortize its organizational costs. Which of the following is considered a qualifying organizational cost?

A. State incorporation fees.

B. Costs for issuing and selling stock or securities.

C. The cost of transferring assets to the corporation.

D. All of the costs are qualifying organizational costs.

66. Which of the following business-related meal expenses would NOT be subject to the 50% rule?

A. A meal incurred while entertaining a business client.

B. A meal while attending a business convention.

C. A meal fully reimbursed to an employee under an accountable plan.

D. A business meal that qualifies as a *de minimis* fringe benefit.

67. Jacob is a 10% partner in Tumbleweed Partnership. In 2011, his beginning partnership basis was $7,000. He received a distribution of $10,000 in cash, plus a car with a partnership basis of $3,000 and a fair market value of $4,500. What is the result of this transaction to Jacob, and how must he recognize the distributions?

A. $3,000 in capital gain; his partnership basis is zero, and his basis in the car is zero.

B. $6,000 in capital gain; his partnership basis is zero, and his basis in the car is $3,000.

C. Zero in capital gain; his partnership basis is (-$3,000), and his basis in the car is $3,000.

D. $4,500 in capital gain; his partnership basis is zero, and his basis in the car is $4,500.

68. When a partnership decides to go out of business and stops all operations and distributes the remaining assets and cash to the partners, this process is called:

A. Consolidation.

B. Liquidation.

C. Closure.

D. Redistribution.

69. On October 1, 2011, Spillway Corporation, a cash-basis, calendar-year corporation, purchases a building, with a $20,000 cash down payment and a mortgage of $30,000. Spillway also pays attorneys' fees of $2,300 to complete the sale. Spillway promptly demolishes the existing building in order to start construction on a new building. The demolition costs are $12,000. What is the basis of the land, and how much can be taken as a current expense in 2011?

A. $50,000 land basis, $14,300 current expense.

B. $52,300 land basis, $12,000 current expense.

C. $62,000 land basis, $2,300 current expense.

D. $64,300 land basis, $0 current expense.

70. Lynden Corporation gives its traveling salespeople $1,000 a month ($12,000 a year) as a car allowance. The salespeople do not have to provide any proof of their car expenses to Lynden Corp. How should these payments be treated?

A. The car allowances are deductible as contractor payments, and they are not taxable to the employees.

B. Lynden Corp. must include the $12,000 on each salesperson's Form W-2. The amounts are not subject to Social Security or Medicare tax.

C. Lynden Corp. must include the $12,000 on each salesperson's Form W-2. The amounts are subject to withholding, as well as Social Security and Medicare tax.

D. The payments can be treated as a gift.

71. The death of a partner has what effect on the partnership?

A. The death of a partner closes the partnership's tax year for that partner.

B. The death of a partner closes the partnership's tax year for the remaining partners.

C. The death of a partner causes an immediate liquidation of partnership assets.

D. The death of a partner is treated as a distribution.

72. Which of the following activities qualifies for the Domestic Production Activities Deduction?

A. Selling food or beverages prepared at restaurants or dining establishments.

B. Software development in the United States.

C. Leasing items to a related party.

D. Customer service businesses.

73. All of the following qualify for a deduction for depletion, EXCEPT:

A. Patents.

B. Timber.

C. Gas wells

D. Mines and natural deposits.

74. The Uniform Capitalization Rules do not apply to any of the following except:

A. Property produced under a long-term contract.

B. Research and experimental expenditures.

C. Loan originations.

D. The production of property for sale to customers.

75. Which form is used to file an estate tax return?

A. Form 1041.

B. Form 706.

C. Form 911.

D. Form 709.

76. Chris became a limited partner in the Patsy Partnership by contributing $12,000 in cash on the formation of the partnership. The adjusted basis of his partnership interest at the end of the current year is $21,000, which includes his $15,000 share of partnership liabilities. At the end of the year, Chris sells his partnership interest for $10,000 in cash. How must Chris report this transaction?

A. He must report $4,000 as a capital gain.

B. He must report $2,000 as a capital loss.

C. He must report $15,000 as a capital gain.

D. He must report $6,000 as a capital gain.

77. During the year, Diamondback Corporation had a $20,000 net operating loss from operations. It also received $100,000 in dividends from a domestic corporation, in which Diamondback holds a 15% stock ownership. There were no other items of income or loss during the year. What is Diamondback's Dividends Received Deduction?

A. $56,000.

B. $80,000.

C. $64,000.

D. $70,000.

78. Which of the following items does NOT decrease an asset's tax basis?

A. The cost of defending a title to the property.

B. A casualty loss.

C. Section 179 accelerated depreciation.

D. A manufacturer's rebate.

79. The Binary Trust is required to distribute all of its income annually. The income and expenses of the trust are shown below. Five hundred dollars of the fiduciary fee is allocated to the tax-exempt interest. How much taxable income will pass through to the trust beneficiaries?

| | |
|---|---|
| • Interest from a Certificate of Deposit | $4,000 |
| • Tax-exempt interest | $2,000 |
| • Fiduciary fee | $1,000 |

A. $3,500.

B. $2,500.

C. $1,500.

D. $5,000.

80. In 2011, Trinity Church had the following activity. What tax return, if any, is Trinity Church required to file?

- Paid $30,000 in wages to three church employees
- Had $800 in Unrelated Business Income (UBIT)
- Received $300,000 in donations from parishioners

A. A church is not required to file a tax return.

B. Trinity must file payroll tax returns and **Form 990-T.**

C. Trinity must file payroll tax returns.

D. Trinity must file **Form 990, Form 941,** and **Form 990-T.**

81. The Las Vegas Rottweiler Rescue qualifies for exempt status as an animal rescue organization. Which form is used by the organization to apply for exemption under IRC Section 501(c)(3)?

A. Form 990.

B. Form 1023.

C. Form 1024.

D. Form 2106.

82. All of the following assets are business related. Which of the following does NOT qualify for a non-taxable 1031 exchange?

A. The exchange of an empty apartment building for farmland.

B. The exchange of partnership interests.

C. The exchange of investment property in one state for the exchange of investment property in another state.

D. The exchange of farm animals of the same sex.

83. Section 1245 property includes all of the following depreciable properties except:

A. Buildings and their structural components.

B. Tangible personal property.

C. A single purpose agricultural structure.

D. Intangible personal property.

84. Philip owns 100% of the stock in Leisure Corporation. In 2011, Leisure Corp. sells a utility van with an adjusted basis of $12,000 and a fair market value of $22,000 to Philip's sister, Gayle, for $11,500. Gayle plans to use the utility van in her business. How must this transaction be reported?

A. Leisure Corp. may take a deductible loss of $500 on the sale of the asset.

B. Leisure Corp. must recognize gain of $500 on the sale of the asset.

C. Leisure Corp. will recognize neither gain nor loss on the sale of the asset.

D. Leisure Corp. may take a deductible loss of $10,500 on the sale of the asset.

85. Derma Corporation is an accrual-basis, calendar-year C Corporation. On December 15, 2011, the board of directors authorizes a charitable contribution of $3,000 to a qualified charity. What is the last day that Derma Corp. can make this charitable contribution and still take the expense on their **2011** tax return?

A. December 15, 2011.

B. December 31, 2011.

C. January 15, 2012.

D. March 15, 2012.

86. Cameo Corporation owned a building that burned down in 2011. The basis of the building before the fire was $240,000. The insurance company reimbursed Cameo Corporation $500,000. How long does Cameo have to reinvest the insurance proceeds in order to get non-recognition treatment for this involuntary conversion?

A. One year from the date of the involuntary conversion.

B. Three years after the year that the involuntary conversion occurred.

C. Two years after the date the involuntary conversion occurred.

D. Three years from the date of the insurance reimbursement.

87. Kristy is a 10% shareholder in Jungle Corp., a C Corporation. She is not an employee of Jungle Corp. The C Corporation loans Kristy $40,000 interest-free for one year. The applicable federal rate at the time of the loan is 7% ($40,000 X 7% = $2,800). How will this transaction be reported, and will Kristy have to recognize any income?

A. Kristy will be forced to recognize $2,800 in imputed interest as dividend income. Jungle Corp. is not allowed a deduction for the dividend paid.

B. Kristy will not be required to recognize any dividend income so long as she repays the loan within the year.

C. Kristy will be forced to recognize $2,800 in imputed interest as dividend income, and Jungle Corp. will be allowed a tax deduction for the dividend paid.

D. Kristy will be forced to recognize $2,800 as taxable wages. Jungle Corp. is not allowed a deduction for the wages paid.

88. What is the maximum amount of startup costs that a business can deduct as a current expense in 2011?

A. $1,000.

B. $5,000.

C. $10,000.

D. $50,000.

89. Which of the following is allowable as a business expense?

A. A political contribution.

B. Lobbying expenses.

C. Repairs to equipment that increase the useful life of an asset.

D. Prepayment penalty on a mortgage.

90. Sam owns Sammy's Sausage Palace. He bought his store building ten years ago, making a down payment of $30,000 and a mortgage of $110,000. Sam paid off the mortgage in six years. He sold the building for $205,000 in 2010. Straight-line depreciation on the building on the date of sale was $22,000. What is the gain on the sale?

A. $43,000.

B. $95,000.

C. $87,000.

D. $153,000.

91. What is the maximum amount of time allowed for an exempt entity to submit its application for exemption, starting with the date of its creation?

A. Four months.

B. Six months.

C. Nine months.

D. Fifteen months.

92. Shania owns a small hair salon as a sole proprietor. During the year she has the following income and expenses:

- Gross receipts $42,000
- Supplies expense $3,500
- Wages for part-time employee $5,000
- Utility expenses $800
- Section 1231 gain $800
- Charitable contribution $1,200

How much business income should Shania report on her **Schedule C?**

A. $53,300.

B. $32,700.

C. $33,500.

D. $32,300.

93. Angie owns a 30% interest in the Günter Partnership. All the general partners share profit and loss according to their ownership stake. There are no limited partners. The partnership reports $90,000 in income for 2011. The partnership distributes $23,000 to Angie in 2011. How much income will Angie recognize on her individual return, and what is the character of the income?

A. $23,000 income, subject to self-employment tax.

B. $23,000 income, not subject to self-employment tax.

C. $27,000 income, subject to self-employment tax.

D. $27,000 income, not subject to self-employment tax.

E. $30,000 income, subject to self-employment tax.

94. In general, which of the following entities is a pass-through entity?

A. S Corporation.

B. Exempt entity.

C. Estate.

D. C Corporation.

95. Which of the following applies only to individual taxpayers?

A. Estimated tax payments.

B. Involuntary conversions.

C. Capital gains.

D. Itemized deductions.

96. During 2011, the Premium Corporation had the following items of income and expense:

| | |
|---|---|
| Income from operations | $50,000 |
| Expenses from operations | $40,000 |
| Dividends received from SAM Corp (a 20% owned corporation) | $120,000 |

Based on the information above, what is Premium Corporation's Dividends Received Deduction?

A. $10,000.

B. $96,000.

C. $104,000.

D. $84,000.

97. Temple Corporation is a fiscal year-end, cash-basis corporation. Temple's tax year ends June 30. When are its estimated taxes due?

A. October 15, December 15, March 15, and June 15.

B. April 15, June 15, September 15, and December 15.

C. March 15, June 15, September 15, and December 15.

D. April 15, June 15, September 15, and January 15.

98. Gloss Corporation is a C Corporation. Gloss Corp. has a net short-term capital gain of $3,000 and a net long-term capital loss of $9,000. The short-term gain offsets some of the long-term loss, leaving a net capital loss of $6,000. The corporation also has $50,000 in ordinary income. Which of the following statements is TRUE regarding this corporation's capital loss?

A. The corporation can use $3,000 of this $6,000 loss to offset ordinary income. The remainder must be carried forward.

B. The corporation treats this $6,000 as a long-term loss that must be carried back for one year and carried forward for up to five years.

C. The corporation treats this $6,000 as a short-term loss that must be carried back for three years and carried forward for up to five years.

D. The corporation treats this $6,000 as a long-term loss that must be carried back for two years and carried forward for up to 20 years.

99. What is the dollar limit of Section 179 depreciation in 2011?

A. $250,000.

B. $350,000.

C. $500,000.

D. $2 million.

100. Driveline Corporation is a calendar-year S Corporation. It has four shareholders:

1. Thomas
2. Ashley
3. Simon
4. Charlotte

The corporation has 10,000 shares outstanding. The shareholders have the following ownership:

| Shareholder | Ownership |
|---|---|
| Thomas | 4,500 shares |
| Ashley | 2,000 shares |
| Simon | 2,000 shares |
| Charlotte | 1,500 shares |
| **Total** | **10,000 shares** |

Charlotte and Thomas wish to terminate Driveline's S-election, but Ashley and Simon do not. What statement is TRUE?

A. Charlotte and Thomas do not have enough stock ownership to terminate the election.

B. All of the shareholders must agree to terminate an S election.

C. Charlotte and Thomas do have enough stock ownership to terminate the election.

D. At least 75% of the shareholders with active ownership must agree to the termination.

Please review your answers with the answers in the back.

# Part 3: Representation Practice Exam

1. Cyril is an Enrolled Agent, and he has a PTIN. Cyril's tax firm employs a bookkeeper named Tania. She gathers client receipts and invoices, and organizes and records all information for Cyril. Cyril prepares all the clients' tax returns and makes all substantive determinations that go into computing the tax liability. Does Tania need a PTIN?

A. No, she is not a tax return preparer and is not required to have a PTIN.

B. Yes, Tania is required to have a PTIN.

C. Tania is a return preparer, but she is not required to have a PTIN because she is an employee.

D. None of the above.

2. In 2011, the IRS instituted an e-file mandate. Most paid preparers are now required to e-file tax returns. If a paid preparer is required to e-file a return, which form is required in order for the tax return to be filed on paper?

A. No additional forms are necessary in order for a paid preparer to file a tax return on paper.

B. Tax returns prepared by a paid preparer, but filed on paper must be submitted with **Form 8948**. A reason must be provided for each return that is not e-filed.

C. Tax returns prepared by a paid preparer, but filed on paper must be submitted with **Form 2848**. A reason must be provided for each return that is not e-filed.

D. New Circular 230 regulations mandate that tax returns prepared by a paid preparer must be e-filed in all circumstances, under penalty of perjury.

3. Which of the following statements is TRUE regarding Registered Tax Return Preparers?

A. If given power of attorney, a Registered Tax Return Preparer may represent a taxpayer only on issues related to the tax return he prepared for that same taxpayer.

B. A Registered Tax Return Preparer may represent a taxpayer before the IRS Examination division and Collection division.

C. A Registered Tax Return Preparer may represent a taxpayer before the Tax Court.

D. A Registered Tax Return Preparer may represent any taxpayer so long as a power of attorney is properly submitted.

4. In the licensing of Enrolled Agents, an "enrollment cycle" refers to ___________?

A. The enrollment year preceding the effective date of renewal.

B. The three successive enrollment years preceding the effective date of renewal.

C. The year in which the Enrolled Agent receives his or her initial enrollment.

D. The amount of continuing professional education required each year of enrollment.

5. Which of the following individuals qualifies as an "enrolled practitioner" under Circular 230?

A. Certified Public Accountant.

B. Enrolled Actuary.

C. Attorney.

D. Unenrolled student volunteers at a VITA site.

E. All of the above.

6. Ethan claimed the EITC (Earned Income Tax Credit) in 2009, 2010, and 2011. He was audited, and the EITC was disallowed in 2011. The IRS also found that Ethan claimed the EITC due to reckless disregard of the EITC rules. Ethan cannot claim the EITC for ______ tax year(s).

A. One.

B. Two.

C. Three.

D. Ethan can never claim the EITC again.

7. Generally, each individual who applies for renewal to practice before the IRS must retain information about Continuing Professional Education hours completed. How long must CPE verification be retained?

A. For one year following the enrollment renewal date.

B. For three years following the enrollment renewal date.

C. For five years if it is an initial enrollment.

D. The individual is not required to retain the information if the CPE sponsor has agreed to retain it.

8. Randall is an accounting student and works for a CPA firm, but he is not a CPA. Randall assists with tax returns but a CPA signs them. Randal is supervised by a licensed CPA. Is Randall required to obtain a PTIN and pass a competency test?

A. Randall needs a PTIN, and he must pass a competency test.

B. Randall needs a PTIN, but he does not need to pass a competency test.

C. Randall does not need a PTIN, and he does not need to pass a competency test.

D. Randall does not need a PTIN and he may sign the returns, so long as he is supervised by a licensed CPA, Enrolled Agent, or attorney.

9. Which form is used to apply for initial enrollment?

A. Form 23.

B. Form 8826.

C. Form 32.

D. Form 5500.

10. What form is used to request innocent spouse relief?

A. Form 8857.

B. Form 2110.

C. Form 8379.

D. Form 8832.

11. Doug Jones recently received his enrollment card, and he wants to purchase new business cards. Which of the following presentations would be acceptable under Circular 230 guidelines?

A. Doug Jones, certified Enrolled Agent.

B. Doug Jones, certified to practice before the Internal Revenue Service.

C. Doug Jones, licensed agent.

D. Doug Jones, enrolled to practice before the Internal Revenue Service.

12. Can multiple individuals in one office share a single PTIN?

A. Yes, multiple preparers may share a single PTIN.

B. Yes, multiple preparers may share one PTIN, but only at the same office location.

C. Yes, multiple preparers may share one PTIN, but only if the principal preparer continues to sign the tax returns.

D. No, each preparer must obtain his or her own PTIN.

13. Which IRS insignia may a tax practitioner use in his or her advertising?

A. The official IRS e-file logo.

B. The U.S. Treasury seal.

C. The IRS eagle insignia.

D. The FMS insignia.

14. What is NOT considered earned income for the purpose of the Earned Income Credit?

A. Non-taxable combat pay.

B. Union strike benefits.

C. Long-term disability benefits received prior to minimum retirement age.

D. Alimony.

15. Which of the following best describes an IRS levy?

A. A levy is not a legal seizure of property.

B. A levy on salary or wages will end when the time expires for legally collecting the tax.

C. A levy can only be released by the filing of a lien.

D. A levy does not apply to the taxpayer's clothing and undelivered mail.

16. Which of the following Taxpayer Number is valid for claiming the Earned Income Credit?

A. Social Security Number.

B. Adoption Taxpayer Identification Number.

C. Individual Tax Identification Number.

D. Employer Identification Number.

17. Which of the following statements regarding e-file is TRUE?

A. E-file providers may charge contingent fees based on a percentage of the refund.

B. Separate fees may be charged for Direct Deposited refunds, so long as the fee is not contingent on the refund amount.

C. E-file providers may charge contingent fees for e-file, but not for paper returns.

D. An e-file provider is required to sign an e-filed return.

18. Which of the following actions is NOT considered "practice before the IRS"?

A. Appearing as a taxpayer's witness before the IRS.

B. Corresponding with the IRS on behalf of a taxpayer.

C. Communicating with the IRS for a taxpayer regarding the taxpayer's rights.

D. Representing the taxpayer at an examination.

19. Which form is used to apply for renewal of enrollment?

A. Form 23.

B. Form 2587.

C. Form 2550.

D. Form 8554.

20. In which of the following situations is an IRS power of attorney required?

A. Allowing the IRS to discuss return information with a third party designee.

B. Allowing a tax matters partner to perform acts for the partnership.

C. Allowing the IRS to discuss return information with a fiduciary.

D. Allowing the tax practitioner to receive, but not cash, taxpayer refund checks.

21. A third party designee has the right to do which of the following tasks?

A. Sign a binding agreement for the taxpayer.

B. Respond to IRS notices about math errors, offsets, and return preparation.

C. Represent the taxpayer before the IRS.

D. Receive refund checks.

22. The IRS may accept an Offer in Compromise based on three grounds. Which of the following is NOT a valid basis for submitting an Offer in Compromise to the IRS?

A. Doubt as to collectability.

B. Effective tax administration.

C. Doubt as to liability.

D. Legitimate hardship argument.

23. Which of the following is considered the most important source of tax law?

A. The United States Code.

B. The Internal Revenue Code.

C. The U.S. Commercial Code.

D. The Congressional Record.

24. Lloyd is an Enrolled Agent. He has a new client, Agnes, who has self-prepared her own returns in the past. Lloyd notices that Agnes has been claiming Head of Household on her tax returns, but she does not qualify for this status, because she does not have a qualifying person. What is Lloyd required to do?

A. Amend the incorrect returns.

B. Refuse any future engagement with this client unless she corrects the prior year returns.

C. Notify Agnes of the error and tell her the consequences of not correcting the error.

D. Notify Agnes of the error and correct the error.

25. Which type of practitioner fee is prohibited by Circular 230?

A. Charging a fee for Direct Deposit.

B. Fixed fees for bookkeeping services.

C. Hourly fee rates for tax consulting

D. Charging a fee for e-filing a return.

26. What form is used for a taxpayer to apply for an Offer in Compromise?

A. Form 656.

B. Form 862.

C. Form 2106.

D. Schedule OIC.

27. Erin wants to split her tax refund into three separate accounts. What is the form she would use in order to notify the IRS of the split refund?

A. Form 8888.

B. Form 8825.

C. Form 1040.

D. Form 2584.

28. For the 2011 tax filing season, which one of the following tax preparers is required to e-file his clients' returns?

A. A paid preparer who anticipates filing 11 or more Forms 1120.

B. A paid preparer who anticipates filing 11 or more Forms 1040.

C. A paid preparer who anticipates filing 11 or more Forms 1065.

D. All of the preparers listed above are subject to the e-file mandate.

29. A tax preparer must complete the paid preparer section of the tax return in which of the following scenarios?

A. An employee preparer who completes employment tax returns for his employer.

B. An Enrolled Agent who prepares her own tax return.

C. A tax professional who prepares a return for her brother and charges him only $30.

D. An Enrolled Agent who prepares his neighbor's return for free.

30. Some returns cannot be e-filed. Of the following, which return may be e-filed?

A. A return that is two years delinquent.

B. An amended return.

C. A tax return where the taxpayer has an ITIN.

D. A tax return where the taxpayer has adopted a child and the child has an ATIN.

31. What is a "Responsible Official" in reference to the IRS e-file application?

A. A Responsible Official is a representative of the IRS that reviews e-file provider applications and approves the provider for acceptance.

B. A Responsible Official is an IRS employee who checks e-file providers for compliance.

C. A Responsible Official is an individual with authority over the e-file provider's operation at a location (usually, he is the owner of the tax practice).

D. A Responsible Official is a Treasury official who is responsible for closing down tax offices that commit fraud.

32. Which of the following is an example of an individual filing a fraudulent or frivolous tax return?

A. A taxpayer who incorrectly claims the Earned Income Credit when he is not eligible for it because he did not read the instructions.

B. A taxpayer who files a return and strikes out the jurat.

C. A preparer who files a return five years late because the taxpayer refused to file.

D. A fiduciary who files an incorrect return and later amends it.

33. Morgan owns a business with five employees. How long is she required to keep employment tax records?

A. Three years.

B. Six years.

C. Five years.

D. Four years.

34. Which of the following disciplinary actions will NOT prevent an Enrolled Agent from practicing before the IRS?

A. Censure.

B. Disbarment.

C. Suspension.

D. None of the above.

36. Which of the following statements is TRUE?

A. The IRS is not required to notify the taxpayer of an audit.

B. In certain circumstances, the IRS may audit tax returns for up to six years after the filing date.

C. Tax returns can only be audited for up to two years after filing.

D. An original tax return that is filed late does not extend the statute of limitations for an audit on the return.

37. How long is an IRS power of attorney authorization valid?

A. A power of attorney is valid until the taxpayer's retirement.

B. A power of attorney is valid for three years.

C. A power of attorney is valid until the close of the taxable year for which it was filed.

D. A power of attorney is valid until revoked.

38. Taxpayers must sign their returns ______________________.

A. Under penalty of perjury.

B. With a physical signature.

C. Before the return has been prepared.

D. Before paying their tax preparer.

39. Tracy is an Enrolled Agent, and she prepares approximately 300 returns for compensation during the year. Which of the following numbers is required in order for her to prepare tax returns for compensation?

A. An Electronic Filing Identification Number (EFIN).

B. A Preparer Tax Identification Number (PTIN).

C. Both A and B.

D. An Employer Identification Number (EIN).

40. Which of the following actions is NOT considered "disreputable conduct" by the IRS?

A. Willfully failing to e-file returns electronically if they fall under the e-filing mandate.

B. Failing to include a valid PTIN on tax returns.

C. Performance as a notary by an enrolled practitioner.

D. Willfully failing to file a tax return.

41. Which of the following statements is TRUE regarding tax practitioners?

A. A tax practitioner is prohibited from charging contingent fees in all cases.

B. A tax practitioner may NOT notarize documents for the clients that they represent before the IRS.

C. A tax practitioner may NOT represent two clients when there is a clear conflict of interest.

D. A tax practitioner is forbidden from discussing tax shelters with a client.

42. Rachel is a CPA. She is taking an aggressive position on a tax return, which requires disclosure. Which form is used to disclose a position on a tax return?

A. Form 8275.

B. Form 8823.

C. Form 656.

D. Form 1040X.

43. Judith, an Enrolled Agent, prepares William's income tax return. William gives Judith power of attorney, including the authorization to receive his federal income tax refund check. Accordingly, the IRS sends William's $1,000 refund check to Judith's office. William is very slow in paying his bills and owes Judith $500 for tax services. Judith should:

A. Use William's check as collateral for a loan to tide her over until William pays her.

B. Refuse to give William the check until he pays her the $500.

C. Get William's written authorization to endorse the check, cash the check, and reduce the amount William owes her.

D. Turn the check directly over to William.

44. Craig is an Enrolled Agent. He wants to request a hardship waiver for an exemption from the electronic filing requirements. Which one of the following statements is true?

A. There is no option for a hardship waiver for paid preparers with the new electronic filing requirements.

B. There is an option for administrative appeal if the IRS denies an e-file hardship waiver request.

C. An e-file waiver will usually be granted automatically, and will be valid until revoked.

D. An e-file waiver may only be requested by paid preparers who can prove financial hardship.

45. Shari is an Enrolled Agent. A client comes in and wants to use Direct Deposit. Which of the following statements is FALSE?

A. Shari must accept any Direct Deposit election to any eligible financial institution designated by the client.

B. Shari may designate refunds for Direct Deposit to up to three qualified accounts.

C. Taxpayers should not request a deposit of their refund to an account that is not in their own name.

D. The taxpayer may designate refunds for Direct Deposit to credit card accounts.

46. What is the penalty for preparers who violate due diligence rules related to the EITC?

A. Any tax return preparer who fails to comply with due diligence requirements for the EITC can be liable for a penalty of $1,000 for each failure.

B. Any tax return preparer who fails to comply with due diligence requirements for the EITC can be liable for a penalty of $500 for each failure.

C. There is no preparer penalty, but there is a taxpayer penalty for fraud.

D. Any tax return preparer who fails to comply with due diligence requirements for the EITC can be formally reprimanded, suspended, or disbarred by the OPR, but there is no monetary penalty.

47. A tax preparer is REQUIRED to provide a copy of the return to a client. Which of the following statements is FALSE?

A. The preparer must provide a complete copy of the return to the taxpayer.

B. A scanned copy of the tax return is sufficient to meet this requirement.

C. The IRS requires that the client receive a paper copy of the tax return.

D. The client copy does not need to contain the Social Security Number of the paid preparer.

48. What is a Private Letter Ruling?

A. It is a private letter that a taxpayer writes to the IRS and that becomes public once tax court litigation begins.

B. It is a private letter issued by the U.S. Tax Court.

C. Private letter rulings are written decisions by the Internal Revenue Service in response to a taxpayer's written request for guidance on a particular tax issue.

D. The Commissioner of the IRS may request a Private Letter Ruling from Congress, in order to clarify Congressional action on a particular tax issue.

49. What is the penalty for filing a frivolous argument with the U.S. Tax Court?

A. Up to $1,000.

B. Up to $5,000.

C. Up to $25,000.

D. Up to $200,000.

50. What is the dollar limit for the U.S. Tax Court small case division?

A. $50,000 or less.

B. $50,000 or more.

C. $15,000 or less.

D. $100,000 or less.

51. Which of the following is NOT a type of Treasury regulation?

A. Legislative regulations.

B. Interpretative regulations.

C. Congressional regulations.

D. Procedural regulations.

52. If an Authorized IRS e-file Provider uses radio, television, Internet, signage, or other advertising methods, which of the following statements is TRUE?

A. The practitioner must keep a copy of the advertising for a minimum of 30 days after the last transmission or use.

B. The practitioner must keep a copy of the advertising until the end of the calendar year following the last transmission or use.

C. The practitioner must keep a copy of the advertising for at least three years following the last transmission or use.

D. The practitioner is not required to keep a copy of advertising.

53. A rejected electronic individual income tax return can be corrected and retransmitted without new signatures if changes do not differ from the amount on the original electronic return by more than:

A. $50 to total income or AGI.

B. $100 of tax due.

C. $50 of tax due.

D. A rejected e-file return cannot be retransmitted without new signatures.

54. In which of the following cases would a taxpayer's federal refund NOT be delayed?

A. Errors in Direct Deposit information.

B. A financial institution refusal of Direct Deposit.

C. Bankruptcy.

D. All of the above may delay a taxpayer's refund.

55. Megan is a CPA, and Alfred is her client. Alfred's e-file return was rejected by the IRS, and Megan is unable to clear the e-file rejection. What is Megan's responsibility, if any?

A. Megan must mail a paper copy of the tax return to Alfred.

B. Megan must take reasonable steps to inform Alfred of the rejection within 24 hours.

C. Megan must take reasonable steps to inform Alfred of the rejection within 48 hours.

D. Megan is not required to notify Alfred of the rejection.

56. What happens when a taxpayer has a late payment on an installment agreement?

A. The late payment on an installment agreement will generate an automatic 30-day notice.

B. The late payment will automatically extend the statute of limitations for collecting the tax.

C. The late payment will cause the installment agreement to default.

D. The IRS will file a Notice of Deficiency.

57. The following individuals are all Enrolled Agents. At the end of 2011, they totaled up their CPE, and this is how many hours each preparer took during the year. Which of them has NOT met the minimum yearly educational requirements for license renewal?

| Preparer | Regular CPE | Ethics CPE |
|---|---|---|
| Francisco | 24 hours | 1 hour |
| Gloria | 16 hours | 2 hours |
| Mona | 14 hours | 4 hours |

A. Francisco.

B. Gloria.

C. Mona.

D. None of these preparers have met their minimum yearly CPE requirement.

58. Natalie became a new Enrolled Agent two years ago. For renewal purposes, which of the following statements is FALSE?

A. Natalie is required to take a minimum of 16 hours of CPE each year.

B. Natalie is required to take a minimum of two hours of ethics CPE per year.

C. Natalie must still fulfill the overall CPE requirement of 72 hours, even though she has only been an EA for two years of the enrollment cycle.

D. For renewal purposes, the annual CPE requirements only apply for the years in which Natalie was an Enrolled Agent.

59. What is the penalty for a preparer who endorses or otherwise cashes a taxpayer's refund check?

A. $100 per occurrence.

B. $500 per occurrence.

C. $1,000 per occurrence.

D. $25,000 per occurrence.

60. A Refund Anticipation Loan (RAL) is a loan between:

A. A taxpayer and a lender.

B. A taxpayer and the IRS.

C. A tax practitioner and the IRS.

D. A lender and the IRS.

61. Which form is used for a taxpayer to request a duplicate copy of his tax return from the IRS?

A. Form 1099.

B. Form 4506.

C. Form 2848.

D. Form 2256.

62. Which of the following statements is FALSE regarding Refund Anticipation Loans?

A. A tax preparer may charge a fee based on the percentage of the refund in exchange for preparing a Refund Anticipation Loan application.

B. The IRS has no responsibility for the payment of any fees associated with the preparation of a return.

C. Tax practitioners must advise taxpayers that RALs are interest-bearing loans.

D. The advertisement on an RAL or other financial product must be in large, readable print.

63. Cherie has a 21-year-old daughter named Abby. Abby's tax return was chosen for examination by the IRS. Cherie is not an Enrolled Agent, attorney, or CPA. Which of the following statements is TRUE?

A. Cherie may represent her daughter before all levels of the IRS if Abby signs a Form 2848.

B. Cherie may not represent her daughter before the IRS because Abby is no longer a minor and Cherie is not enrolled to practice before the IRS.

C. Cherie may represent her daughter because she is not a trained tax accountant.

D. A parent may not represent a child because of privacy regulations.

64. The "Statutory Notice of Deficiency" is also known as:

A. A 30-day letter because the taxpayer generally has 30 days from the date of the letter to file a petition with the Tax Court.

B. A 90-day letter because the taxpayer generally has 90 days from the date of the letter to file a petition with the Tax Court.

C. An Information Document Request (IDR) because the taxpayer is asked for information to support its position regarding liability for tax.

D. A federal tax lien.

65. Enrolled Agents have a limited confidentiality privilege for communications with their clients. Which of the following statements is FALSE regarding the confidentiality protection between an Enrolled Agent and his tax client?

A. The confidentiality protection for certain communications between a taxpayer and an attorney applies to similar communications between a taxpayer and any federally authorized tax practitioner.

B. The confidentiality protection applies to all non-criminal tax matters before the IRS.

C. The confidentiality privilege extends to any administrative proceeding with any other federal agency.

D. The confidentiality privilege does not apply to the promotion of the direct or indirect participation of a corporation in a tax shelter.

66. Which of the following statements is TRUE about Registered Tax Return Preparers?

A. A Registered Tax Return Preparer is only permitted to prepare and sign tax returns, and may not appear before the IRS examination division.

B. A Registered Tax Return Preparer may not appear as a witness before the IRS.

C. A Registered Tax Return Preparer is allowed to receive tax refund checks on a client's behalf.

D. A Registered Tax Return Preparer is eligible to represent a taxpayer only about a tax liability arising from a tax return prepared for that individual.

67. Which of the following actions is a Registered Tax Return Preparer allowed to perform?

A. Negotiate payment arrangements.

B. Argue the validity of an assessment.

C. File an extension of time to file a tax return.

D. Request adjustments to an account.

68. Tax practitioners may not base their fees on ________________________.

A. Time spent on preparing individual returns.

B. A percentage of the refund amount.

C. A set fee for preparation of an individual form.

D. A flat fee for certain types of returns.

69. The Director of the Office of Professional Responsibility has instituted a disciplinary proceeding against Barbara, an Enrolled Agent. Barbara fails to respond to the complaint. Which of the following statements is FALSE?

A. The failure to respond constitutes an admission of guilt and a waiver of the hearing.

B. The administrative law judge may make a decision on the case by default without a hearing or further procedure.

C. Barbara does not have the right to appeal the administrative law judge's decision if she fails to appear or respond to the complaint.

D. During a hearing, the practitioner may be represented by an attorney or another practitioner.

70. Jeff was an Enrolled Agent. He was recently disbarred from practice during his hearing with an administrative law judge. Jeff wants to appeal the judge's decision. Where would he file his appeal after this initial hearing?

A. The Secretary of the Treasury.

B. The Office of Professional Responsibility.

C. The Internal Revenue Service Examination Division.

D. The U.S. Tax Court.

71. A "Covered Opinion" is which of the following?

A. Written advice given to an employer by a full-time employee.

B. The preparation of delinquent returns.

C. Written advice prepared for a taxpayer after the tax return has been prepared.

D. Written advice a practitioner gives a client regarding a tax shelter.

72. In which of the following cases does an IRS power of attorney expire or terminate?

A. When the client becomes incapacitated.

B. When the client leaves the country.

C. When the practitioner changes office locations.

D. When the client dies.

73. An ERO may originate the electronic submission of tax returns by:

A. Electronically sending the return to a Transmitter that transmits the return to the IRS.

B. Directly transmitting the return to the IRS.

C. Providing a return to an Intermediate Service Provider for processing prior to transmission to the IRS.

D. All of the above are allowable procedures for transmitting an electronic return.

74. In which of the following situations must the tax preparer obtain permission from the client to disclose sensitive tax return information?

A. The preparer receives a grand jury subpoena requesting client records.

B. A 10% general partner in a partnership requests copies of the partnership return.

C. An executor requests copies of a return for a deceased taxpayer's estate.

D. None of the above.

75. Robin is an Enrolled Agent. She has two clients who have recently divorced, and there is a clear conflict of interest between both parties. How should Robin proceed?

A. Robin may represent both of her clients so long as the conflict of interest is disclosed in writing to both parties and both parties agree.

B. Robin may represent both of her clients so long as the conflict of interest is disclosed to at least one party and he or she agrees.

C. Robin may not represent either client if a clear conflict of interest exists.

D. Robin may only represent one of the clients if a clear conflict of interest exists. The other client must be dismissed.

76. How often do Enrolled Agents renew their enrollment?

A. Every three years.

B. Every five years.

C. Every year.

D. None of the above.

77. For which of the following reasons would the Office of Professional Responsibility NOT accept a CPE waiver?

A. Health issues.

B. Active deployment for military personnel.

C. Absence from the United States for employment or other reasons.

D. Because the tax practitioner did not receive his or her enrollment renewal.

78. Which of the following statements is FALSE regarding an IRS power of attorney?

A. A newly filed power of attorney concerning the same matter will revoke a previously filed power of attorney.

B. The filing of Form 2848 will not revoke any Form 8821 (Document Information Authorization) that is in effect.

C. A signed Form 8821 is sufficient for a practitioner to represent a taxpayer before the IRS.

D. A power of attorney held by a student of a Low Income Tax Clinic is valid for only 130 days from the received date and will automatically be revoked.

79. What is the Taxpayer Advocate Service?

A. A private tax litigation firm.

B. A branch of the U.S. Tax Court that helps resolve taxpayer issues.

C. An independent organization within the IRS to help taxpayers resolve problems with the IRS.

D. A state agency designed to ensure federal and state compliance with current tax laws.

80. Alana owes $5,000 to the IRS, but she cannot pay in full. She applies for a payment plan by completing Form 9465, *Installment Agreement Request*. What is the maximum number of months that she can request to pay off her balance?

A. 12 months.

B. 24 months.

C. 60 months.

D. No maximum, so long as she continues to make her minimum payments on time.

81. The Freedom of Information Act (FOIA) does not require the IRS to release all documents that are subject to FOIA requests. The IRS may withhold information:

A. Due to budget cuts.

B. Due to the statute of limitation for FOIA requests.

C. If the requester fails to provide notarized identification along with the request.

D. For an IRS record that falls under one of the FOIA's nine statutory exemptions or by one of three exclusions under the Act.

82. Don is an Enrolled Agent. He sent out an advertisement announcing a flat rate of $100 for preparation of a single tax return. Don later changes his mind and wants to increase the price. Don is bound by this advertised rate for a minimum of ________ days after the last date on which the fee schedule was published:

A. 20 days.

B. 30 days.

C. 45 days.

D. 60 days.

83. Which of the following statement is FALSE about the IRS and court cases?

A. The IRS must respect and follow the decisions of every court case.

B. The IRS may choose to appeal any court decision other than a decision by the Supreme Court.

C. The IRS publishes its acquiescence and non-acquiescence in the Internal Revenue Bulletin.

D. The IRS does not announce acquiescence or non-acquiescence in every case.

84. What is the mission of the Office of Professional Responsibility (OPR)?

A. The Office of Professional Responsibility is duty-bound to license enrolled practitioners.

B. The Office of Professional Responsibility establishes and enforces consistent standards of competence, integrity, and conduct for tax professionals and other individuals and groups covered by IRS Circular 230.

C. The Office of Professional Responsibility provides small businesses top quality service by educating and informing them of their tax obligations, developing educational products and services, and helping them understand and comply with applicable laws.

D. The Office of Professional Responsibility provides America's taxpayers with top quality service by helping them to understand their tax responsibilities and by enforcing the law with integrity and fairness to all.

85. Which of the following facts regarding Revenue Rulings is FALSE?

A. Revenue Rulings *can* be used to avoid IRS penalties.

B. Revenue Rulings *cannot* be used to avoid IRS penalties.

C. A Revenue Ruling is an official interpretation by the IRS of the Internal Revenue Code.

D. A Revenue Ruling can be challenged in court.

86. Which of the following sanctions will the Office of Professional Responsibility NOT impose on a practitioner?

A. Permanent disbarment.

B. Sanctions.

C. Formal reprimand.

D. Criminal penalties.

87. Which of the following disputes may not be resolved by a proceeding in the U.S. Tax Court?

A. Gift tax.

B. Income tax.

C. Employment taxes.

D. Innocent spouse relief.

88. An IRS power of attorney must contain all of the following information EXCEPT:

A. The type of tax involved.

B. The name and address of the representative.

C. The name and Social Security Number of the taxpayer.

D. The specific date the tax return was filed, if delinquent.

89. A paid preparer is required by law to ______________________.

A. Charge a fee for e-filing.

B. Sign the return and fill in the preparer areas of the form.

C. Include his Social Security Number on the tax return.

D. None of the above.

90. Webster is an Enrolled Agent, and he wants to apply to become an authorized e-file provider. Which of the following is NOT a requirement to become an IRS e-file provider?

A. To be a United States citizen or a legal U.S. alien lawfully admitted for permanent residence (a "green card" holder).

B. To be at least 21 years old as of the date of application.

C. To have a permanent business location *outside* his or her home, in order to ensure the safety of client confidentiality and client records.

D. To meet applicable state and local licensing or bonding requirements for the preparation and collection of tax returns.

91. The IRS must give a taxpayer reasonable notice before contacting third parties in connection with examinations or collecting tax liability. However, the IRS is not required to give notice in which of the following instances?

A. Any pending criminal matter.

B. When providing notice would jeopardize collection of any tax liability.

C. When providing notice may result in reprisal against any person.

D. When the taxpayer authorized the contact.

E. All of the above.

92. Enrolled Agents are allowed a limited confidentiality privilege with their clients. Confidential communications do not extend to:

A. Non-criminal tax matters before the IRS.

B. Non-criminal tax proceedings brought in court.

C. Correspondence audits.

D. Tax shelter opinions.

93. Which of the following statements is FALSE?

A. A taxpayer is prohibited from recording his meeting with an IRS auditor unless the taxpayer is represented by an Enrolled Agent, CPA, or tax attorney.

B. A taxpayer may record the examination interview with the IRS.

C. The request to record the examination meeting should be made in writing.

D. A taxpayer must notify the IRS ten days in advance in order to record an examination.

94. The IRS offers fast track mediation for all of the following issues EXCEPT:

A. Examinations (audits).

B. Offers in Compromise.

C. Trust fund recovery penalties.

D. Cases that are docketed in the district court.

95. Penny has an installment agreement in place with the IRS. In March 2011, she gets into a bad car accident and misses a payment. The IRS sends her a notice 30 days later and terminates her installment agreement. Which of the following statements is FALSE?

A. Penny has no appeal rights once the installment agreement is in default.

B. The IRS can't levy until 30 days after the termination of an installment agreement.

C. If Penny appeals within a 30-day period after the termination, the IRS will be prohibited from levying until her appeal is completed.

D. Penny may call the telephone number shown on the notice and explain that she wants to appeal the termination.

96. Which of the following statements regarding the IRS Collection Appeals Program (CAP) is FALSE?

A. A taxpayer cannot appeal a CAP hearing decision to the U.S. Tax Court.

B. The CAP process is generally quicker and is available for a broader range of collection actions.

C. A Low Income Tax Clinic may represent taxpayers who qualify.

D. A taxpayer may go to court if he disagrees with the CAP decision.

97. Trent decided to represent himself in an IRS audit. When he arrived at the IRS office, he became agitated during the initial examination interview and requested to speak to a representative. Which of the following statements is correct?

A. The taxpayer may leave the examination and finish the audit through correspondence.

B. An IRS interview must be suspended when the taxpayer clearly requests the right to consult with a representative.

C. If the taxpayer chooses to suspend the interview, he must return in person with his representative.

D. The IRS is not required to cease an examination when the taxpayer requests a representative.

98. What is a CP-2000 notice?

A. A CP-2000 notice shows proposed changes to a taxpayer's income tax return.

B. A CP-2000 notice demands a payment from a taxpayer.

C. A CP-2000 notice shows proposed changes to a taxpayer's examination.

D. A CP-2000 notice alerts the taxpayer of an impending IRS examination.

99. If there is substantial unreported income (over 25%), the IRS may audit tax returns for up to __________ after the filing date.

A. Three years.

B. Five years.

C. Six years.

D. Indefinitely.

100. Juanita is an Enrolled Agent. Her client, Clive, had his return rejected. Clive will be given ______ from the date of a rejected return to resubmit the return, even if the submission is made after the due date of the return.

A. 24 hours.

B. 5 days.

C. 10 days.

D. 30 days.

Please review your answers with the answers in the back.

# Test Answers

# Individuals: Answers

**1. The answer is C.** Youssef must complete **Form 982** in order to report the cancellation of debt. Although there is a loss, it cannot be deducted. The mortgage debt cancellation is not included in income on the taxpayer's return because it is covered by the Qualified Principal Residence Indebtedness Exclusion on **Form 982.**

**2. The answer is B.** Generally, a passive activity is any rental activity OR any business in which the taxpayer does not materially participate. Non-passive activities are businesses in which the taxpayer works on a regular, continuous, and substantial basis. In addition, passive income does not include salaries, portfolio, or investment income. Income and losses from the following activities generally would be considered passive: equipment leasing, rental real estate, and operation of a farm (or any other business) in which the taxpayer does not actually participate. There are two exceptions to this passive activity loss limitation. First, businesses in which the taxpayer materially participates are not considered "passive activities." Second, although rental income is generally considered passive income, there is an exception in the law for real estate professionals.

**3. The answer is A.** The nanny is a household employee. Household employees include housekeepers, maids, babysitters, gardeners, and others who work in or around a taxpayer's private residence as employees. If an employer pays a household employee wages of less than $1,700 in 2011, the employer does not have to report and pay Social Security and Medicare taxes on that employee's wages. The $1,700 threshold is the same as 2010. For more information, see Social Security and Medicare wages in **Publication 926**, *Household Employer's Tax Guide*.

**4. The answer is C.** Employees use **Form 2106** to deduct ordinary and necessary expenses related to their job. An employee can use Form 2106 to deduct expenses that were not reimbursed by his employer. (Amounts included in box 1 of the employee's **Form W-2** are not considered reimbursements, because those amounts have been taxed as regular wages.)

**5. The answer is D.** A PTIN is a Preparer Tax Identification Number that is used by preparers only, not by taxpayers. There are only three types of Taxpayer Identification Numbers: the Social Security Number (SSN), the Adoption Taxpayer Identification Number (ATIN), and the Individual Tax Identification Number (ITIN). An Employer Identification Number (EIN) is used by entities, not by individuals.

**6. The answer is C.** In 2011, the amount of taxable investment income a child can have without it being subject to tax at the parents' rate is $1,900. This amount is unchanged from 2010. Children with investment income may have the income taxed at their parents' tax rate rather than at the child's rate. Investment income includes interest, dividends, capital gains, and other unearned income. This rule does not apply to wages; it applies to passive income only. To figure the child's tax using the parents' rate for the child's return, the taxpayer must fill out **Form 8615,** *Tax for Certain Children Who Have Investment Income of More Than $1,900*, and attach it to the child's income tax return. For more information, see **Publication 929,** *Tax Rules for Children and Dependents.*

**7. The answer is C.** If the taxpayer does not receive his **Form W-2** in order to file timely, the taxpayer may use **Form 4852**, which is a "substitute" W-2 form. If necessary, taxpayers may use pay stubs, bank records, prior year forms, or other information to estimate the **Form W-2** data.

**8. The answer is B.** Gambling losses may be claimed as a miscellaneous itemized deduction, <u>not subject</u> to the 2% floor, on **Schedule A.** However, the amount of losses deducted *may not exceed* gambling winnings. A taxpayer can only deduct gambling losses if he itemizes deductions. For more information, see **Publication 529,** *Miscellaneous Deductions*.

**9. The answer is A.** A taxpayer can include in medical expenses the costs of buying, training, and maintaining a guide dog or other service animal to assist a visually-impaired or disabled person. For more information, see **IRS Publication 502,** *Medical and Dental Expenses Including the Health Coverage Tax Credit.* Take the time to review the "allowable" medical expenses in **Publication 502**. There will always be one or two questions on the EA exam related to this subject.

**10. The answer is A**. Reggie can include in medical expenses the entire amount he paid. Amounts paid to buy and install special plumbing fixtures for a person with a disability, mainly for medical reasons, in a rented house, are deductible medical expenses, according to IRS **Publication 502**. The rules are slightly different when the medical improvements are done on a house that the taxpayer owns. Review IRS Publication 502 for the differences, or the PassKey EA Review section that deals with medical expenses and itemized deductions (Part 1).

**11. The answer is C.** Because Gary paid more than half the cost of keeping up his mother's apartment from January 1 until her death and he can claim an exemption for her, he can file as Head of Household.

**12. The answer is C.** A taxpayer may be eligible to file as Head of Household if the dependent who qualifies the taxpayer for this filing status is born or dies during the year. Even if a child lives for a very short time, he or she may still be claimed as a dependent. The child must be born alive. Stillborn births do not qualify. There must be proof of a live birth shown by an official document such as a birth certificate. Under these unique circumstances, if the taxpayer does not have a Social Security Number for the child, the taxpayer may attach a copy of the child's birth certificate and death certificate instead and enter "DIED" on **Form 1040**. This is a very special exception, and it is outlined in **Publication 17.** The tax return cannot be e-filed and must be submitted on paper with a copy of the birth certificate and the death certificate.

**13. The answer is B**. His father must apply for an Individual Taxpayer Identification Number (ITIN), and then Rodrigo can claim his father as a dependent. If a dependent is a resident or non-resident alien who is not eligible to get an SSN, he must apply for an ITIN by using **Form W-7**, *Application for IRS Individual Taxpayer Identification Number*. In order for a taxpayer to claim a dependency exemption for someone, a residency test must be met. To meet the "citizen, national, or resident test," an individual must be a citizen of the United States, a resident of the United States, or a citizen or resident of Canada or Mexico. For more information, see **Publication 501**.

**14. The answer is A.** In 2011, anyone can make a qualified rollover contribution to a Roth IRA regardless of the taxpayer's modified AGI. If a taxpayer wants to convert a traditional IRA to a Roth IRA, he is required to pay federal income taxes on any pretax contributions, as well as any growth in the investment's value. Once the funds are converted to a Roth, all of the investment grows tax-free, and funds can be withdrawn on a tax-free basis. Although there are still income limits to who can *participate* in a Roth IRA, beginning with tax year 2010, anyone may convert an existing traditional IRA to a Roth IRA. For more information, see **Publication 17.**

**15. The answer is A.** Abel does not have a deductible casualty loss. The loss deduction is figured as follows:

| Loss after insurance | $2,000 |
|---|---|
| Subtract $100 | $100 |
| Loss after $100 rule | $1,900 |
| Subtract 10% × $29,500 AGI | $2,950 |
| **Theft loss deduction** | **$–0–** |

Abel does not have a theft loss deduction because his loss after applying the $100 rule ($1,900) is less than 10% of his adjusted gross income ($2,950). Each personal casualty or theft loss is limited to the excess of the loss over $100 (instead of the $500 limit that applied for 2009). In addition, the 10%-of-AGI limit continues to apply to the net loss in most cases. For more information, see **Publication 17**.

**16. The answer is D.** Because Greg does not meet the age test, Sandy's son is not her qualifying child. Because he does not meet the gross income test, Greg is not her qualifying relative. As a result, he is not Sandy's qualifying person for Head of Household purposes. For more information, see **Publication 501**.

**17. The answer is B.** Dianne can file as Head of Household because John did not live with her for the last six months of the year.

**18. The answer is D.** Daniel and Maria may take three exemptions on their tax return. Daniel can take a personal exemption for himself and, since he is married, one for his spouse. They can also take an exemption for Daniel's stepmother. If a taxpayer's qualifying person is a dependent parent, the taxpayer may still take a dependency exemption even if the parent does not live with the taxpayer.

**19. The answer is D.** Suzy must file MFS, and she will also be forced to itemize. On an MFS return, if one spouse itemizes deductions, the other spouse must also itemize and cannot claim the standard deduction. Suzy also cannot claim the dependency exemption for Sam, because she is not the custodial parent. If the parents separated during the year and the child lived with both parents before the separation, the custodial parent is the one with whom the child lived for the greater number of nights during the rest of the year. Neither spouse qualifies for Head of Household, because they did not separate until September 2011. For more information, see **Publication 501**.

**20. The answer is B.** A non-resident alien who is married to a U.S. citizen does not automatically get treated as a resident for tax purposes. An election can be made by both spouses to treat a non-resident spouse as a U.S. resident for tax purposes. All of the other answers are taxpayers who would automatically be treated as U.S. residents for income tax purposes. Aliens are considered residents for tax purposes if they are lawful permanent residents of the United States (holders of green cards) at any time during the calendar year, regardless of their domicile. Individuals holding green cards have automatic U.S. resident status unless it is taken away from them or is administratively or judicially determined to be abandoned.

**21. The answer is C.** Chad provided more than half of his own support for the year. Therefore, he is not Harold's qualifying child or his qualifying relative. To meet the Support Test, the child cannot have provided more than half of his own support for the year. For more information, see **Publication 17**.

**22. The answer is C.** Only Aaron qualifies for the Child Tax Credit. A qualifying child for this credit must be **under** age 17 and a U.S. citizen or national or a U.S. resident. For purposes of the Child Tax Credit, a child must:

- Be a son, daughter, stepchild, foster child, brother, sister, stepbrother, stepsister, or a descendant of any of them (for example, a grandchild, niece, or nephew);
- Be under age 17 at the end of 2011;

- Have not provided over half of his or her own support for 2011;
- Have lived with the taxpayer for more than half of 2011;
- And be a U.S. citizen, a U.S. national, or a U.S. resident alien.

For more information, see **Publication 972,** *Child Tax Credit.*

**23. The answer is D.** Gambling income does NOT qualify as earned income for the purpose of the EIC. For the purpose of the EIC, earned income includes wages and self-employment income. Taxable earned income also includes:

- Wages, salaries, and tips
- Union strike benefits
- Long-term disability benefits received prior to minimum retirement age
- Net earnings from self-employment
- Combat pay

The taxpayer can elect to have non-taxable combat pay included in earned income for the Earned Income Credit.

**24. The answer is C.** The maximum amount of investment income he can have and still get the EITC credit is $3,150 for 2011.

**25. The answer is A.** Melanie turned 13 on May 1 and is no longer a qualifying person for the purposes of this credit. For the Child and Dependent Care Credit, the child must be under the age of 13 (or be disabled, of any age). Ray can use the $2,000 of expenses for Melanie's care January through April (before she turned 13) to figure his credit because it is not more than the $3,000 yearly limit. For more information, see **Publication 503**, *Child and Dependent Care Expenses*.

**26. The answer is A.** The other answers are incorrect. A foster child may be treated just like a biological child for the purposes of the Earned Income Tax Credit. A child is an eligible foster child if the child is placed with the taxpayer by an authorized placement agency or by judgment, decree, or other order of any court.

**27. The answer is A.** Francesca's filing status is Single. Unlike divorce, an annulment is retroactive. If a taxpayer obtains a court decree of annulment, which holds that no valid marriage ever existed, the taxpayer is considered unmarried even if he or she filed joint returns for earlier years. The taxpayer must file amended tax returns claiming Single or Head of Household status (if applicable) for each tax year affected by the annulment that is not closed by the statute of limitations for filing a tax return. The statute of limitations generally does not end until three years after the original return was filed.

**28. The answer is C.** Eligible educators can deduct up to $250 of qualified expenses as an adjustment to income. The deduction is claimed on either line 23 of Form 1040 or line 16 of **Form 1040A**. If the taxpayer and spouse are both educators, they can deduct up to $500, but neither can deduct more than their first $250. For courses in health and physical education, expenses are deductible if they are related to athletics. Teachers can deduct these expenses even if they do not itemize deductions. Previously, educator expenses were deductible only as a miscellaneous itemized deduction (subject to the 2% of adjusted gross income limit). Only certain teachers qualify. An eligible educator must work at least 900 hours a school year in a school that provides elementary or secondary education (K-12). College instructors do not qualify. The term "educator" includes:

- Teacher
- Instructor
- Counselor
- Principal
- Teacher's aide

Any excess expenses may be treated as an itemized employment-related deduction on **Schedule A.**

**29. The answer is D.** Rebecca is a statutory non-employee. Big House properly issues Rebecca a **Form 1099 MISC** for commissions and Rebecca files a **Schedule C** to report her income and expenses. There are generally two categories of statutory non-employees: direct sellers and licensed real estate agents. They are treated as self-employed for all federal tax purposes, including income and employment taxes, if:

- Substantially all payments for their services as direct sellers or real estate agents are directly related to sales or other output, rather than to the number of hours worked, and
- Their services are performed under a written contract providing that they will not be treated as employees for federal tax purposes. (See **Publication 15-A**, *Employer's Supplemental Tax Guide.*)

**30. The answer is D.** The maximum amount of wages subject to Social Security tax for 2011 is $106,800. There is no limit on the amount of wages subject to Medicare tax. In most cases, employees in the United States must pay Social Security and Medicare taxes. The employee's payment of these taxes contributes to the individual's coverage under the U.S. Social Security system.

**31. The answer is B.** Any amount that is reduced due to a contingency related to the child (such as the child dying, getting married, or going to school) is considered by the IRS to be child support, rather than alimony. Child support payments are neither deductible by the payer nor taxable to the payee.

**32. The answer is D.** The Adoption Credit is refundable in 2011. The other credits listed are all non-refundable.

**33. The answer is A.** Debt cancellation that occurs prior to the filing of bankruptcy does not qualify for the exclusion. However, canceled debts may be excluded from taxable income if the debts are forgiven as part of a Title 11 bankruptcy proceeding. The debt must be discharged through bankruptcy and not before the filing. There are many other examples of non-taxable debt cancellation, and in order to make yourself familiar with these complex rules, you should read **Publication 4681,** *Canceled Debts, Foreclosures, Repossessions, and Abandonments*.

**34. The answer is B.** All of the income is taxable except the inheritance. Amounts received in the form of gifts or inheritances are not included in taxable income.

**35. The answer is C.** Tina, as the child's parent, will be the only one allowed to claim her son as a qualifying child for the Earned Income Credit. The IRS will disallow her mother's claim to the dependency exemption. Tina cannot file as Head of Household, however, because she did not pay any of the costs of keeping up the home. Tie-breaker rules: to determine which person can treat the child as a qualifying child, if only one of the persons is the child's parent, the child will be treated as the qualifying child of the parent.

**36. The answer is B.** Steve cannot claim the Earned Income Credit. As a non-custodial parent, he does not meet the residency test because the child did not live with him. Only a custodial parent can claim the Earned Income Credit based on a dependent child. Refer to **Publication 596,** *Earned Income Credit,* for the Earned Income Credit rules. If the non-custodial parent qualifies to claim the dependency exemption for a child, he *may* claim the Child Tax Credit if the other requirements for claiming the credit are met. The Child Tax Credit can only be claimed by the parent claiming the dependency exemption.

**37. The answer is B.** If a taxpayer earned over $1,500 in interest or dividend income, he is required to report the earnings on Schedule B and attach it to **Form 1040**. For more information, see **Publication 550,** *Investment Income and Expenses.*

**38. The answer is C.** Janice must file a **Schedule C** for the restaurant showing her net profit of $25,000 and Marty must file his own Schedule C for the catering business showing his net loss of $1,500. Janice's **Schedule SE** will show total earnings subject to SE tax of $25,000. Even if taxpayers file a joint return, they cannot file a joint **Schedule SE**. This is true whether one spouse or both spouses have earnings subject to self-employment tax. Married taxpayers cannot use losses from each other's businesses to offset self-employment tax. However, if an individual taxpayer operates multiple businesses, he must combine the net profit (or loss) from each to determine total earnings subject to SE tax. A loss from one business reduces the profit from another business. So, for example, if Janice had been running two businesses, then the loss from the second business would have reduced her overall profit and also her self-employment tax. For more information, see **Publication 334,** *Tax Guide for Small Business.*

**39. The answer is D.** All of the charges are deductible as mortgage interest. Their mortgage interest deduction is $14,370 ($12,200 + $50 + $120 +$2,000). Taxpayers can deduct a late payment charge on a mortgage loan as mortgage interest. Sometimes, if a person pays off his home mortgage early, he must pay a penalty. The taxpayer can deduct a prepayment penalty as home mortgage interest provided the penalty is not for a specific service performed or cost incurred in connection with the mortgage loan. When taxpayers sell their home, they may deduct home mortgage interest paid up to, but not including, the date of the sale. For more information, see **Publication 936,** *Home Mortgage Interest Deduction.*

**40. The answer is C.** Victoria may claim $26,400 in alimony paid as an adjustment to income on her individual **Form 1040,** the total of the medical expenses and the regular alimony paid ($15,000 + $11,400). Alimony paid is an adjustment to income, and is claimed on page 1 of **Form 1040**. A taxpayer does not need to itemize deductions in order to claim an adjustment for alimony paid. The payor can deduct the full amount because it is all **required** by the divorce agreement. Alimony is a payment to or for a spouse or former spouse under a divorce or separation agreement. Alimony does NOT include voluntary payments that are not made under a divorce or separation decree. Payments to a third party (such as the payment directly to the hospital) on behalf of an ex-spouse under the terms of a divorce or separation agreement can qualify as alimony. These include payments for an ex-spouse's medical expenses, housing costs (rent, utilities, etc.), taxes, and tuition. The payments are treated as received by the spouse and then paid to the third party. For more information, see **Publication 504**, *Divorced or Separated Individuals.*

**41. The answer is B.** Laverne can deduct $4,500, subject to the 2% limit, as a miscellaneous itemized deduction. Legal fees for a divorce are not a deductible expense. However, because a taxpayer must include alimony received in gross income, she can deduct legal fees related to the collection of alimony. In addition, a taxpayer may deduct fees paid to appraisers, actuaries, and accountants for tax advice or for services related to the determination of correct tax. An individual taxpayer can deduct these legal fees only if she itemizes deductions on **Schedule A (Form 1040)**. They are reported as a miscellaneous itemized deduction subject to the 2%-of-Adjusted-Gross-Income limit. For more information, see **Publication 504**, *Divorced or Separated Individuals.*

**42. The answer is A.** Kayla meets the support test because she did not provide half of her own support. The support test determines the level of support by the child, not the person who wants to claim the child as a dependent. Children generally cannot have provided more than half of their own support during the tax year. A person's own funds are not support unless they are *actually spent* for support.

**43. The answer is C.** In order to qualify for the Earned Income Credit, the taxpayer cannot file **Form 2555** or **Form 2555-EZ** (which excludes foreign earned income). None of the other examples would exclude a taxpayer from claiming the EITC. Choice A is incorrect because resident aliens (green card holders) are generally taxed the same way as American citizens. Aliens are considered residents for tax purposes if they are lawful permanent residents of the United States (holders of green cards) at any time during the calendar year. Choice B is incorrect because Head of Household filing status does not disqualify a taxpayer from claiming the EITC. Choice D is incorrect because taxpayers are allowed to file a joint return with a deceased spouse in the year of death.

**44. The answer is D.** The amounts for loss of wages and emotional distress are taxable as ordinary income ($4,000 + $10,000 = $14,000). The damages awarded for physical injury are not taxable. Damages for emotional distress are usually taxable, except for any amounts that were paid for medical care related to the emotional distress (such as a person who is treated for depression after an incident).

**45. The answer is B**. Sarah can claim a refund of the Social Security taxes withheld from the last $3,200 in earnings when she files her 2011 personal income tax return. When a person works more than one job in a year, each of the employers is required by law to withhold Social Security taxes from the wages without regard to what other employers may have withheld. The taxpayer may then end up with total Social Security taxes withheld that exceed the maximum. For more information, refer to **Publication 505**, *Tax Withholding and Estimated Tax.*

**46. The answer is C.** The Adoption Credit is refundable in 2011. Gabrielle may claim an adoption credit of $13,360.

**47. The answer is C.** An employee can generally exclude $5,000 from an employer-financed Flexible Spending Account. However, if a taxpayer is filing MFS, the maximum he can exclude is $2,500. Benefits that are in excess of those limits ($5,000/$2,500 for MFS) are included in gross income. Terry cannot take the Dependent Care Credit for any of the remaining amounts because in order to claim the credit for child and dependent care expenses, the taxpayer's filing status must be Single, Head of Household, Qualifying Widow(er), or Married Filing Jointly. For more information, see **Publication 503**, *Child and Dependent Care Expenses.*

**48. The answer is A.** These expenses are deductible on **Schedule A** as a miscellaneous itemized deduction, subject to the 2% floor. They are deductible because they relate to Matt's investment activity. The tax code allows for a deduction for the production or collection of income, such as the management of investments. Since investing is not a self-employment activity (unless a person is a bona fide securities dealer), then the costs related to this activity such as the safe deposit box and the subscriptions to the investing magazines would not go on **Schedule C**. For more information, see **Publication 550,** *Investment Income and Expenses.*

**49. The answer is C.** Tom may choose to take a lump sum distribution or start taking minimum distributions from the retirement plan. The distribution will be subject to income tax, but it will NOT be subject to the 10% early withdrawal penalty. He cannot roll over the inherited retirement plan into his own existing plan. The IRS generally imposes a 10% early withdrawal penalty on early distributions (distributions before the age of 59½). However, there are many exceptions to this rule, and one is when the original owner of the plan dies. Since Tom was Leigh's son, he cannot choose to roll over the amounts into his own plan (only surviving spouses have the option to do that). Current tax law allows a beneficiary of an inherited IRA to choose between taking a full distribution immediately, which is taxable, or continue tax-deferred growth and take minimum annual distributions over his lifetime. The rules regarding IRAs and pension plans are very complex and heavily tested on Part 1 and Part 2 of the EA exam. Take the time to study the rules for the exam because you can expect numerous questions related to this subject. See **Publication 590,** *Individual Retirement Arrangements,* for additional information.

**50. The answer is D**. The Smiths must report the amount that was credited to their mutual fund account, regardless of the amount that was actually distributed to them. The amounts from a mutual fund are always reported as a long-term capital gain regardless of how long someone has held the shares. Investors may have to pay taxes on any capital gains distribution they receive — even if the fund went on to perform poorly after they bought shares. That's because the law requires mutual funds to distribute capital gains to shareholders if they sell securities for a profit that can't be offset by a loss. For more information, see **Publication 564,** *Mutual Fund Distributions.*

**51. The answer is D.** Ellen's at-risk amount for this activity includes all her costs, investment, and the debt that she personally absorbs for the business. Since Ellen used her own credit cards for the purchase of business materials, this is also considered an investment in her business. If any of the debt had been non-recourse, then an individual is not considered at-risk for amounts that are protected from loss through non-recourse financing.

**52. The answer is B.** Generally, the expenses of renting a property, such as maintenance, insurance, taxes, and interest, can be deducted from the rental income. If a taxpayer owns a "partial interest" in rental property, he can deduct expenses paid according to the percentage of ownership. The cost is a repair, not an improvement, because the window was broken. If all the windows had been replaced with energy-efficient windows, then that would have been considered an improvement and would have been added to the property's basis. For more information, see **Publication 527,** *Residential Rental Property.*

**53. The answer is A.** The American Opportunity Credit is a maximum credit of up to $2,500 for the cost of qualified tuition and related expenses paid during the taxable year for each eligible student. Taxpayers receive a tax credit based on 100% of the first $2,000 of tuition, fees, and course materials paid, plus 25% of the next $2,000 of qualified expenses paid. This is a per-student limit. The expenses for Lynette do not qualify, because the American Opportunity Credit can only be claimed for expenses for the first four years of post-secondary education. The American Opportunity Credit is partially refundable in 2011. For Lynette's expenses, Ursula may be able to take the Lifetime Learning Credit instead.

**54. The answer is D.** This is a "trick" question, and variations have been on prior exams. The full amount of $5,000 is taxable to Clark because the IRS stipulates that if a student is not a degree candidate, all financial aid is subject to federal income tax, even if it is spent on educational expenses. For more information, see **Publication 970**, *Tax Benefits for Education.*

**55. The answer is B.** Because David's new job location is 57 miles farther from his former home than the distance from his former home was to his old job location, he meets the distance test. A move will meet the distance test if the new main job location is *at least 50 miles* farther from the former home than the old job location was from the former home. For example, if the old job location was three miles from the former home, the new main job location must be at least 53 miles from that former home. Deductible moving expenses include moving household goods and personal effects (including in-transit or foreign-move storage expenses), and traveling (including lodging but NOT meals) to a new home. A taxpayer can include the cost of storage and insuring household goods within any period of 30 consecutive days before or after the moving day. ***Note:** Make sure that you study the concept of the "Time Test" and the "Distance Test" in your PassKey study guide or in the IRS publications. You should be prepared to answer questions regarding moving expenses and the deductibility of expenses and how to qualify for the Moving Expense Deduction. For more information, see **Publication 521**, *Moving Expenses*.

**56. The answer is B.** Individuals who have been physically present for at least 183 days over a three-year period, including the current year, meet the requirements of the substantial presence test. This includes 183 days over a three-year period comprising the current year (must be at least 31 days); one-third of the days in the first year before the current year; and one-sixth of the days in the second year before the current year. The rules define residency for tax purposes in a way that is very different from immigration laws. Although the immigration laws of the United States refer to aliens as immigrants, non-immigrants, and undocumented (illegal) aliens, the **tax laws** of the United States refer only to RESIDENT and NON-RESIDENT ALIENS. In general, the controlling principle is that RESIDENT ALIENS are taxed in the same manner as U.S. citizens on their worldwide income, and NON-RESIDENT ALIENS are taxed according to special rules contained in certain parts of the Internal Revenue Code. A major distinguishing feature of this special tax treatment concerns the source of income: a non-resident alien is subject to federal income tax only on income that is derived from sources within the United States and/or income that is effectively connected with a U.S. trade or business. On the other hand, a taxpayer that meets residency tests for the U.S. will be taxed on worldwide income. For more information, see **Publication 519,** *U.S. Tax Guide for Aliens.*

**57. The answer is B**. Ramon can claim Head of Household status since his spouse is a nonresident alien who will not file a joint return with him, and he meets all the other qualifications for Head of Household. There is a special exception in the tax code that allows U.S. citizens and resident alien spouses who live with their non-resident alien spouses to file as Head of Household. All of the following requirements must be met:

- The taxpayer is a U.S. citizen or resident alien for the entire year and meets all the rules for Head of Household except for living with the non-resident alien spouse.
- The non-resident alien spouse does not meet the substantial presence test.
- The non-resident alien spouse does not choose to file a joint return.

For more information, see **Publication 519**, *U.S. Tax Guide for Aliens.*

**58. The answer is B.** Since their combined gross income is $16,000 (which is under $21,300), Carol and Javier do not have to file a return. They do not qualify for the Earned Income Credit because they are both over 65 years old. (This "age test" only applies to taxpayers without any qualifying children.)

**59. The answer is C.** Self-employed individuals generally are required to file an annual return and pay estimated tax quarterly. A taxpayer is required to file an income tax return if net earnings from self-employment are $400 or more.

**60. The answer is D.** If a taxpayer must file a U.S. tax return or is listed on a tax return as a spouse or dependent, and does not have and cannot obtain a valid SSN, the taxpayer must apply for an ITIN.

**61. The answer is B.** Taxpayers should keep the supporting documentation for their tax returns for at least three years from the date the return was filed, or two years from the date the tax was paid, whichever is later. This also includes applicable worksheets, receipts, and other forms. For more information see **Publication 552,** *Recordkeeping for Individuals.*

**62. The answer is B.** Alice's original basis per share was $11 ([$1,050 + $50 broker's commission= $1,100] ÷ 100). After the stock dividend, her $1,100 basis must be spread over 110 shares (100 original shares plus the additional 10 shares). Therefore, if Alice's basis in the stock was $1,100 for 100 shares, the ten additional shares mean Alice's basis per share decreased to $10 per share ($1,100 ÷ 110). This is the concept of a "stock dividend," and this is often tested on the EA exam. Make sure you review all the information about stock sales, basis, and stock dispositions in your study guide. For additional information, see **Publication 551,** *Basis of Assets.*

**63. The answer is C.** Both taxpayers must file. Taxpayers who are under 65, using the Married Filing Separately status, and earn at least $3,700 are required to file a return.

**64. The answer is A.** Although Lenny owned the ten shares he received as a non-taxable stock dividend for only three months, all the stock has a long-term holding period. Stock acquired as a stock dividend has the same holding period as the original stock owned. Because he bought the stock for $1,500 three years ago, his holding period is long term. Lenny has a long-term capital gain of $530 on the sale of the 510 shares.

**65. The answer is B.** Nora does not need to itemize in order to claim the adjustment for the penalty on early withdrawal of savings. The deduction can be claimed on **Form 1040** or **Form 1040A**. She cannot use Form **1040EZ.**

**66. The answer is C**. If a child of divorced or separated parents is claimed as a dependent on either parent's return, each parent may deduct the medical expenses they individually paid for the child. This is a special exception for divorced and separated individuals. For more information, see **Publication 502**, *Medical and Dental Expenses*.

**67. The answer is A.** This is a trick question! Harvey is over the age limit for a traditional IRA contribution. On the other hand, if Harvey was under the age of 70½, Married Filing Separately, he could contribute no more than his $2,000 compensation. Also be aware that there is no age limit for Roth IRA contributions. Make sure you read up on all the IRA contribution rules for the EA exam. Be very cautious and read exam questions carefully.

**68. The answer is D.** Non-prescription and over-the-counter drugs are not deductible as a medical expense on Schedule A. Taxpayers may deduct transportation related to medical care. The cost of prescription drugs and acupuncture are also deductible. For more information, see **Publication 502**, *Medical and Dental Expenses.*

**69. The answer is B.** Colleges provide a **Form 1098-T** to the taxpayer to report the total amount of eligible tuition and fees paid during the tax year.

**70. The answer is C.** Olga's total itemized deduction for taxes is $4,000 ($2,000 + $1,900 +$100 = $4,000). The $250 homeowners' association fee is not deductible. All the other costs are deductible as taxes. For more information, see **Publication 600**, *State and Local General Sales Taxes* and **Publication 17,** *Your Federal Income Tax.*

**71. The answer is A.** Keith and Tiffany can deduct the interest on their loans because the total of these loans throughout 2011 ($72,000) does not exceed $100,000, and the total amount of the home equity loan ($72,000) is not more than the home's fair market value minus any outstanding acquisition debt ($230,000 - $30,000 = $200,000). For more information, see **Publication 936,** *Home Mortgage Interest Deduction.*

**72. The answer Is B.** Hana's distribution was not made after the 5-year period beginning with the first taxable year she made a contribution to her Roth IRA. Therefore, only the return of her regular contributions is not included in her gross income. Any earnings would be taxable. She would also have to report the withdrawal on **Form 8606**, *Non-deductible IRAs*, even though portions of the withdrawal might not be taxable. Distributions from a Roth IRA are tax-free and may be excluded from income if the following requirements are met:

- The distribution is made after the 5-year period beginning with the first taxable year for which a contribution was made to a Roth IRA, AND the distribution is:
  - Made on or after age 59½, or
  - Made because the taxpayer was disabled, or
  - Made to a beneficiary or to an estate, or
  - To pay certain qualified first-time homebuyer amounts (up to a $10,000 lifetime limit)

**73. The answer is C.** In the case of charity volunteers, transportation expenses, including bus fare, parking fees, tolls, and either the cost of gas and oil or a standard mileage deduction of 14 cents per mile can be deductible as an itemized deduction on Schedule A. Raffle tickets (or any type of gambling expense) are never deductible as a charitable contribution, even if the event directly benefits a charity. Blood donations are not deductible, but the cost of travel to make a blood donation is a deductible expense. A taxpayer cannot deduct a donation that is made directly to a needy individual.

**74. The answer is B.** Sonny's share of partnership income should be reported on **Schedule E, Form 1040. Schedule E** is used to report income or loss from rental real estate, royalties, partnerships, S Corporations, estates, trusts, and residual interests in REMICs. A taxpayer must attach **Schedule E** to his **Form 1040** in order to report income or loss from any of these sources. Partnerships use **Schedule K-1** to report each partner's share of the partnership's income, deductions, credits, etc. Although the partnership is not subject to income tax, taxpayers are liable for tax on their share of the partnership income. Partnerships are tested on Part 2 of the EA exam, but for Part 1 you will need to know how to report the partner's distributive share of income on his individual return. Schedule K-1s are not filed with the tax return. Taxpayers should keep **Schedule K-1s** with their records.

**75. The answer is B.** The $30,000 in debt cancellation is treated as a reduction in basis in the property and should be reported on **Form 982**. The debt cancellation is covered by the Qualified Principal Residence Indebtedness Exclusion and is not counted as taxable income on the return. **Form 8949** and **Schedule D** are not required because Paloma did not dispose of the home.

**76. The answer is B.** Mai Lin may only deduct $15,000 ($25,000 - [50% x $20,000]) of the rental losses in the current year. Taxpayers who actively participate in a rental real estate activity can deduct up to $25,000 of loss from the activity from non-passive income. But the $25,000 allowance is phased out if modified adjusted gross income (MAGI) is between $100,000 and $150,000. The $25,000 limit gets phased out by $1 for every $2 that the taxpayer earns over $100,000. If the taxpayer's MAGI is $150,000 or more ($75,000 or more if Married Filing Separately), there is no special allowance. This special allowance is an exception to the general rule disallowing losses in excess of income from passive activities. For more information, see **Publication 527**, *Residential Rental Property.*

**77. The answer is A.** Only a taxpayer who was active duty military on extended duty can still qualify for the First Time Homebuyer Credit. The initial credit for qualified buyers is equal to 10% of the purchase price of the principal residence, with a maximum credit of $8,000 ($4,000 for married individuals filing separately). The deadline for making qualifying purchases in 2011 was July 1, 2011. The taxpayer had to have entered into a written binding contract before May 1, 2011.

**78. The answer is C.** Raymond is allowed to rollover his traditional IRA into a government deferred-compensation plan (section 457 plan).Taxpayers are allowed rollover their traditional IRA to any of the following plans without incurring tax or penalty:

- A rollover into another traditional IRA
- A qualified plan
- A tax-sheltered annuity plan (section 403(b) plan)
- A Government deferred-compensation plan (section 457 plan)

IRAs cannot be held jointly, so spouses are not allowed to rollover funds into each other's retirement plans. However, a taxpayer is allowed to rollover an IRA from a *deceased* spouse. After death, the surviving spouse may elect to treat the IRA as his own, and roll it over into another traditional IRA.

**79. The answer is B.** The sales price was $4,400, which was $1,900 more than the original basis of $2,500 ($2,400 cost + $100 commission) of the shares. The broker's commission would be deducted when figuring the amount of gain. The gain is the difference between the sales price and the adjusted basis.

**80. The answer is B.** The adjusted basis of the house at the time of the change in its use was $182,000. The basis for depreciation on the house is the fair market value on the date of the change ($147,000), because it is less than Carlos's adjusted basis ($182,000). When a primary residence is changed to rental use, the basis for depreciation will be the lesser of fair market value or adjusted basis on the date of conversion. Land is not subject to depreciation. For more information, see **Publication 527**, *Residential Rental Property*.

**81. The answer is B.** On Kyle's tax return, he can deduct $3,000 of the capital loss. The unused part of the loss, $4,000 ($7,000 – $3,000), can be carried over to the following year. Kyle's adjusted gross income is $29,000 ($32,000 – $3,000 capital loss). Capital losses can be deducted on a taxpayer's return and used to reduce other income, such as wages, up to an annual limit of $3,000, (or $1,500 if Married Filing Separately).

**82. The answer is A.** In general, the deadlines for performing certain actions applicable to his taxes are extended for the period of Kevin's service in the combat zone, plus 180 days after his last day in the combat zone. This extension applies to the filing and paying of his income taxes that would have been due April 15 (or April 17 in 2012). During his extension period, assessment and collection deadlines will be extended, and he will not be charged interest or penalties attributable to the extension period.

**83. The answer is B.** The donor is generally responsible for paying the gift tax. A gift is not taxable to the recipient. The annual exclusion for gifts made to a donee during 2011 is $13,000, unchanged from 2010. The general rule is that any gift over $13,000 is a taxable gift. However, there are many exceptions to this rule. Generally, the following gifts are not taxable gifts:

- Gifts that are not more than the annual exclusion ($13,000 in 2011).
- Tuition or medical expenses paid for someone directly to a college or a medical provider (the educational and medical exclusions).
- Gifts to a spouse who is a U.S. Citizen.
- Gifts to a political organization for its own use.

**84. The answer is B.** Josh and Larissa may each make a maximum contribution of $5,000 to a traditional IRA. This is because Josh, who has no compensation, can add Larissa's compensation, reduced by the amount of her IRA contribution ($50,000 – $5,000 = $45,000) to his own compensation ($0) to figure his maximum contribution to a traditional IRA. For more information, see **Publication 590,** *Individual Retirement Arrangements*.

**85. The answer is C.** A taxpayer can deduct the expenses of:

- Moving household goods, pets, and personal effects (including in-transit or foreign-move storage expenses), and
- Traveling (including lodging but NOT meals) to a new home.

In order to be deductible, the moving expenses must have been paid or incurred in connection with starting work at a new job location. For more information, see **Publication 521,** *Moving Expenses*.

**86. The answer is B.** The maximum amount taxpayers may claim for the non-refundable Child Tax Credit is $1,000 for each qualifying child. The amount actually claimed on Form 1040 depends on the taxpayer's tax liability, modified adjusted gross income (MAGI), and filing status. This credit is phased out once MAGI reaches the following income levels:

- Married Filing Jointly - $110,000
- Single, Head of Household, or Qualifying Widow(er) - $75,000
- Married Filing Separately - $55,000

**87. The answer is B.** Chelsea has a taxable gain of $30,000. Her basis in the new home is $80,000. The part of her gain that is taxable is $30,000 ($130,000 – $100,000), the unspent part of the payment from the insurance company. The rest of the gain ($20,000) is not taxable, because it was reinvested into the replacement home. This follows the rules for involuntary conversions (IRC Section 1033). The basis of the new home is figured as follows.

| | |
|---|---|
| Cost of replacement home | $100,000 |
| Minus: Gain not recognized | ($20,000) |
| Basis of the replacement home | $80,000 |

For more information, see **Publication 523**, *Selling Your Home.*

**88. The answer is C.** Chuck can exclude up to $250,000 of gain on a separate or joint return for 2011. The $500,000 maximum exclusion for joint returns does not apply because Jayme does not meet the "use test." For more information, see **Publication 523**, *Selling Your Home.*

**89. The answer is A.** There is a special rule known as the "15-Day Rule" for homes that are rented for fewer than 15 days a year. In this case, the rental income is not reported. The mortgage interest on a second home or a vacation home is deductible on Schedule A. For more information, see **Publication 527,** *Residential Rental Property* (which includes the rental of vacation homes).

**90. The answer is C.** Wilson's office is 20% (240 ÷ 1,200) of the total area of his home. Therefore, his business percentage is 20%. His expenses for the year were $12,000 ($1,000 per month x 12 months) and $600 ($50 x 12 months). The answer is figured as follows:

$12,000 total rent

<u>$600 total utilities</u>

$12,600 total expenses for the year X 20% (business use percentage) = $2,520. For more information, see **Publication 587,** *Business Use of Your Home*.

**91. The answer is D.** Angel's deductible expense would be calculated as follows: $300 + $245 + $150 + $30 ($60 X 50%) = $755. All of the expenses are qualifying expenses, but the meal expense must be reduced by 50%. Employees can deduct work-related educational expenses as a miscellaneous itemized deduction on Form 1040, Schedule A; the expense is subject to the 2% of adjusted gross income limit. For more information on educational expenses, refer to **Publication 970,** *Tax Benefits for Education*.

**92. The answer is D.** Taxpayers can deduct the cost and upkeep of uniforms, if the uniforms are not suitable for everyday use. (Taxpayers cannot deduct the cost of regular clothing used for work.) The clothing must be specifically required by the employer. Scott can only claim the amount of expenses that exceeds 2% of his adjusted gross income. The expense is deductible on Schedule A (Form 1040) as a miscellaneous itemized deduction, subject to the 2% floor. For more information on work-related expenses and miscellaneous deductions, see **Publication 529,** *Miscellaneous Deductions*.

**93. The answer is A**. The value of the free use of a taxpayer's property is not a charitable deduction. Qualified contributions must be made in cash or property. For more information, see **Publication 526**, *Charitable Contributions.*

**94. The answer is A.** The casualty loss is figured as follows:

| | |
|---|---|
| Basis of property | $4,000 |
| Minus | ($100) (*the $100 Rule) |
| Allowable loss | $3,900 |
| Less 10% of $24,000 AGI | ($2,400) (*the 10% Rule) |
| **Audrey's loss deduction** | **$1,500** |

Individuals are required to claim their casualty losses as an itemized deduction on Form 1040, Schedule A. For property held for personal use (not business-use property), the taxpayer must subtract $100 from each casualty that occurred during the year. Then add up all those amounts and subtract 10% of adjusted gross income from that total to calculate the allowable casualty and theft losses for the year. For more information, see **Publication 547**, *Casualties, Disasters, and Thefts*.

**95. The answer is A.** The credit amount limit for windows in 2011 is 10%, up to $200. The 2011 credit for windows is limited to a combined limit for all tax years after 2005 of $200. The Residential Energy Property Credit increases the energy tax credit for homeowners who make energy efficient improvements to their existing homes. This credit applies to improvements such as adding insulation, energy-efficient exterior windows, and energy-efficient heating and air conditioning systems.

**96. The answer is A.** Unlike a traditional IRA, Roth IRAs do not require minimum distributions at age 70½. For more information, refer to **Publication 590**, *Individual Retirement Arrangements (IRAs).*

**97. The answer is D.** Gregory has a wash sale, and he cannot take the capital loss. In general, a wash sale occurs when a taxpayer sells stock or other securities at a loss and, within 30 days before or after the sale or disposition, the taxpayer buys or acquires substantially identical stock or securities. The wash sale rules also apply if a taxpayer sells stock and then the taxpayer's spouse immediately buys identical stock. Since Gregory's wife purchased identical securities within 30 days after Gregory sold his stock, he has a wash sale. It doesn't matter that he and his wife file separate tax returns, because the wash sale rules still apply. Gregory's $4,000 loss is instead added to the cost basis of the new stock. The result is an increased basis in the new stock. This adjustment postpones the loss deduction until the disposition of the new stock or securities. The holding period for the new stock includes the holding period of the stock or securities sold.

**98. The answer is D.** For income tax purposes, Pastor Green excludes $31,000 from gross income ($24,000 fair rental value of the parsonage plus $7,000 from the allowance for utility costs). He will report $60,000 as regular income ($59,500 salary plus $500 of unused utility allowance). His income for SE tax purposes, however, is $91,000 ($67,000 salary + $24,000 fair rental value of the parsonage). Services that a duly ordained, commissioned, or licensed minister performs in the exercise of his ministry are generally covered under the Self-Employment Contributions Act. That means the minister is exempt from Social Security and Medicare withholding, but the minister is then responsible for paying self-employment tax on his net earnings from self-employment. The fair rental value of a minister's parsonage (also called a housing allowance) is excludable from income only for income tax purposes. No exclusion applies for self-employment tax purposes. For more information, refer to **Publication 517**, *Social Security and Other Information for Members of the Clergy and Religious Workers*.

**99. The answer is B.** Theo's gross profit percentage is 12.5% ($15,000 ÷ $120,000). Theo would report 12.5% of each payment, (12.5% x $30,000) = $3,750), as installment sale income from the sale for the tax year he receives the payment (after subtracting interest, if any). The remainder (balance) of each payment is the tax-free return of his adjusted basis. For more information, refer to **Publication 537,** *Installment Sales*.

**100. The answer is C.** The taxpayer is not required to request an EIN if he operates multiple businesses, as long as those businesses are all sole proprietorships without employees. The taxpayer WILL need an EIN if any of the following are true:

- He files bankruptcy under Chapter 7 (liquidation) or Chapter 11 (reorganization)
  of the Bankruptcy Code.
- He incorporates or takes in partners to operate as a partnership.
- He is establishing a pension, profit sharing, or retirement plan.
- He files employment or excise tax returns.

He will NOT need a new EIN if any of the following are true:

- He changes the name of his business.
- He changes the location or adds locations (stores, plants, enterprises, or branches of the same entity).
- He operates multiple businesses (including stores, plants, enterprises, or branches of the same entity).

For more information, refer to **Publication 334**, *Tax Guide for Small Business*.

# Businesses: Answers

**1. The answer is C.** Since Davenport Corporation operates on the accrual basis, then it must meet the "all events test" and "economic performance" must have occurred before deducting and/or accruing the expense. Davenport is not required to pay the expense first. Under the accrual method of accounting, transactions are reported (and accrued) as they occur, regardless of when the actual cash (or other method of payment) is actually received or paid.

**2. The answer is B.** The accumulated earnings tax is assessed on the accumulated earnings and profits of a C Corporation. If a corporation allows earnings to accumulate beyond the reasonable needs of the business, it may be subject to an accumulated earnings tax of 15%. The IRS imposes this tax upon corporations with retained earnings deemed to be "unreasonable" and in excess of what is considered ordinary. The accumulated earnings tax does not apply to partnerships, sole proprietorships, or S Corporations, because these businesses are pass-through entities and do not accumulate earnings from year to year, as a C Corporation does. For more information, see **Publication 542**, *Corporations*.

**3. The answer is B.** The IRS only allows an employer to provide $50,000 of term life insurance coverage tax-free to the employee. There are no tax consequences if the total amount of the life insurance policy does not exceed $50,000. The value of any coverage over this amount must be included in wages and reported on Form W-2. The employer must calculate the taxable portion of the premiums for coverage that exceeds $50,000. For more information, see **Publication 15-B**, *Employer's Tax Guide to Fringe Benefits*.

**4. The answer is C.** The first corporate tax return is due March 15 of the following year. This short period return covers May 15, 2011 through December 31, 2011. Corporate tax returns are due on the fifteenth day two-and-a-half months after the end of the corporation's taxable year. Since the corporation elected the calendar year, then the corporate return is due two-and-a-half months after the end of December.

**5. The answer is D.** A non-profit entity (exempt organization) must file **Form 990**, NOT **Form 1120**. In order for an entity to qualify as exempt, it must be organized as a community chest, corporation, trust, fund, or foundation (**Publication 526**). A non-profit entity may still be classified as a corporation, but its income is non-taxable (exempt), and it is required to file a non-profit tax return, which is IRS **Form 990**.

**6. The answer is B**. If liabilities assumed by the corporation exceed the basis of the assets transferred, then the relief from liabilities in excess of basis is treated as boot. In the case of a Section 351 exchange, a taxpayer will not recognize any gain or loss in the transfer, so long as the following conditions are met:

- The taxpayer receives ONLY stock in exchange for the property, and
- The taxpayer has a controlling interest in the corporation immediately after the exchange. In order to qualify, the taxpayer must have at least 80% ownership in corporate stock.

**7. The answer is A.** A family farming corporation may use the cash method of accounting if its average annual gross receipts are $25 million or less. A tax shelter must always use the accrual method, regardless of its gross receipts. A corporation with long-term contracts must always use the accrual method. A C Corporation with gross receipts exceeding $5 million must use the accrual method of accounting.

**8. The answer is B.** A domestic LLC that has at least two members and does not file a **Form 8832** will automatically be classified by the IRS as a partnership for tax purposes.

**9. The answer is C.** The maximum Section 179 deduction the company can claim for 2011 is $355,000 ($100,000 for the equipment + $5,000 computer + $250,000 for the qualifying leasehold improvements). In 2011 there is a special rule that allows taxpayers to deduct a maximum of $250,000 of Qualified Real Property (QRP) under Section 179. The taxpayer must elect to treat QRP as Section 179 property. This special provision only applies to certain industries and property types and includes the following real property:

- Qualified leasehold improvement property.
- Qualified restaurant property (improvements to a restaurant building, such as a major renovation.)
- Qualified retail improvement property (for example, an improvement of a retail clothing store, including major interior upgrades and other similar improvements.)

The maximum amount of Section 179 expenses for QRP is limited to $250,000 (although a business is still eligible to deduct the full $500,000 limit for other qualifying property).

**10. The answer is C.** U.S. payers of income other than wages (royalties, etc.) are required to withhold tax on income paid to non-resident aliens at a flat rate of 30%. Generally, a foreign person is subject to U.S. tax on its U.S. source income. Most types of U.S. source income received by a foreign person are subject to U.S. tax of 30%. A reduced rate, including an exemption, may apply if there is a tax treaty between the foreign person's country of residence and the United States. Most American allied nations have a favorable tax treaty in place (including Australia, most of Europe, Canada, and Mexico). The tax is generally withheld automatically from the payment made to the foreign person. For more information, see **Publication 515**.

**11. The answer is D.** The partnership must include the fair market value (FMV) of the items it received in exchange for services. This is bartering income, and it is treated as though the partnership had received money. Therefore, the answer is $8,000 + $3,000 = $11,000.

**12. The answer is B.** Because they used the car 70% for business, they can deduct 70% of the expenses as a business expense. The answer is figured as follows:

($235 + $20 + $25) = $280 X 70% = $196
($5,500 x 70%) = $3,850
Allowable expense: $4,046
For more information, see **Publication 334**, *Tax Guide for Small Businesses.*

**13. The answer is A.** Its final return is due by October 15, 2011 and will cover the short period from January 1, 2011 through July 22, 2011. The return is due on the fifteenth day of the third month after the close of its taxable year. In this case, the taxable year ended on the date the entity was dissolved. This is called a "short year" tax return. Even if a taxable entity was not in existence for the entire year, a tax return is required for the time it was in existence. Requirements for filing a "short year" return and figuring the tax are generally the same as the requirements for a return for a full tax year (12 months) ending on the last day of the short tax year.

**14. The answer is D.** A partnership is not liable for self-employment tax. However, the individual partners themselves would be liable for self-employment tax on their portion of the earnings from the partnership. A partnership can be liable for employment taxes if the partnership has employees. A partnership can be liable for late filing penalties on delinquent partnership or payroll tax returns. A partnership may have to pay excise taxes. Excise taxes are special taxes on specific goods—such as gasoline, tobacco, or firearms. A business that sells or uses these products may be required to pay excise taxes on them. For more information, see **Publication 334,** *Tax Guide for Small Businesses.*

**15. The answer is C.** A sole proprietorship with 100 employees is not required to file electronically. The IRS requires partnerships with more than 100 partners (Schedules K-1) to electronically file their return. A small tax-exempt organization that wishes to file **Form 990-N** must file electronically, as there is no paper version of this form available. Corporations that have assets of $10 million or more and file at least 250 returns annually are required to electronically file **Forms 1120** and **Form 1120S** (this applies to S Corporations and C Corporations).

**16. The answer is A.** A private foundation is always required to file an annual information return, regardless of its income or loss for the year. A church, government entity, or an organization that is a subordinate of a parent organization (and included on the parent organization's return) is not required to file an annual information return. For more information, see **Publication 1828**, *Tax Guide for Churches and Religious Organizations.*

**17. The answer is B.** The general rule is that an expense paid in advance is deductible only in the year to which it applies. The expense for the business insurance must be prorated because the payment does not qualify for the 12-month rule. Therefore, only $500 (6/36 × $3,000) is deductible in 2011, $1,000 (12/36 × $3,000) is deductible in 2012, $1,000 (12/36 × $3,000) is deductible in 2013, and the remaining $500 is deductible in 2014. To read more about the 12-month rule, check your PassKey study guide or read IRS **Publication 538,** *Accounting Periods and Methods*.

**18. The answer is A. Form 8829**, *Expenses for Business Use of Your Home*, is used to calculate and report home office expenses.

**19. The answer is D.** Cash and cash equivalent fringe benefits (for example, use of a gift card, charge card, or credit card), are not excludable as a de minimis benefit, except for occasional meal money or transportation fare. For more information, see **Publication 15-B**, *Employer's Tax Guide to Fringe Benefits*.

**20. The answer is B.** Participant loans are NOT permitted. Participants are always 100% vested in (in other words, have ownership in) all of the funds in their IRAs. Withdrawals are permitted anytime, but they are subject to income taxes (except for certain distributions from non-deductible IRAs and Roth IRAs). If the employee is under age 59½, there may also be a 10% penalty tax. With an IRA, the employees control where their money is invested, and they also bear the investment risk. The financial institution holding the IRA manages the funds. An employee may also move IRA assets from one IRA provider to another. For more information, see **Publication 4587,** *Payroll Deduction IRAS for Small Businesses*.

**21. The answer is C.** The entire meal amount is a qualified expense, but subject to the 50% meal and entertainment limitation. The taxpayer can deduct the full amount of the travel in the taxi cab. Therefore, the deductible portion of the expense is figured as follows: ($250 X 50%) + $10 =$135.

**22. The answer is B.** The corporation does not recognize any income or loss from this exchange. However, Manny (now the majority shareholder) must recognize ordinary income of $13,000 as payment for services he rendered to the corporation. If a taxpayer transfers property (or money) to a corporation in exchange for stock and immediately gains control of the corporation, the exchange is usually not taxable. This non-recognition treatment does not apply when a person exchanges *services* for stock. In order to be "in control" of a corporation, the taxpayer who transfers the property must own, immediately after the exchange, at least 80% of the stock. For more information, see **Publication 542**, *Corporations.*

**23. The answer is B.** Cheryl may not deduct the taxes as a current expense, since they are delinquent real estate taxes and the person who is legally liable for the debt is Alex. However, the taxes should be added to the property's basis and depreciated as part of the purchase price, since Cheryl intends to use the property as a rental. If a taxpayer agrees to pay the delinquent real estate taxes that the seller owes on real property, the buyer must treat those taxes as part of the asset's basis. The buyer cannot deduct them as taxes. For more information, see **Publication 551**, *Basis of Assets.*

**24. The answer is A.** Harrington's basis in the new plane is $70,000 (the $30,000 basis of the old plane plus the $40,000 paid). The FMV of the new plane has no bearing on the basis in a Section 1031 exchange. If a business trades property in a qualified "like-kind" exchange and also pays money, the basis of the property received is the basis of the property given up, increased by the additional money paid. For more information, see **Publication 551**, *Basis of Assets.*

**25. The answer is C.** A new corporation establishes its tax year when it files its first tax return. Businesses must file **Form 1128** to adopt, change, or retain a tax year. The IRS will grant automatic approval to any C corporation so long as the entity has not changed its accounting period in the previous 48 months. If the business does not qualify for *automatic* approval, a ruling must be requested, and a user fee must be paid. For more information, see **Publication 538,** *Accounting Periods and Methods.*

**26. The answer is D.** The cost of shipping finished products to customers are not product costs and not part of the Cost of Goods Sold (COGS) calculation. However, "freight-in" costs are part of the cost of goods calculation. There are several factors that go into determining COGS, including inventory at the beginning of the year; raw material purchases; direct labor costs (generally applies to manufacturing and mining operations); materials and supplies; other costs; and inventory at the end of the year. Starting inventory, net purchases, cost of labor, materials and supplies, and other costs are added together. Inventory at the end of the year is subtracted from this total to determine COGS. For more information, see **Publication 334**, *Tax Guide for Small Business.*

**27. The answer is B.** Currently, U.S. tax law requires businesses to submit a Form 1099 for every contractor paid at least $600 for services during a year. This requirement does not apply to corporations receiving payments.

**28. The answer is A.** Mario's basis is the cash he contributed, and Juan's basis is his adjusted basis in the property. The FMV does not affect the basis of the partner's interest. The basis of a partnership interest is the money (cash investment) PLUS the adjusted basis of any property the partner contributed. For more information, see **Publication 541,** *Partnerships*.

**29. The answer is B.** A non-resident alien cannot hold shares in an S Corporation. All of the other entities would be permitted to be shareholders in an S Corporation. Shareholders in an S Corporation must be U.S. citizens or residents. Corporate shareholders and partnerships are excluded. However, certain trusts, estates, and tax-exempt corporations, most notably 501(c)(3) corporations, are permitted to be shareholders.

**30. The answer is C.** A guaranteed payment must actually be paid to the partner in order to be classified as a "guaranteed payment." Guaranteed payments are those made by a partnership to a partner that are determined without regard to the partnership's income. In other words, the payments will be made, even if the partnership loses money. In this respect, these payments are treated as though they are being made to an outsider.

**31. The answer is B.** The basis of Karen's partnership interest is $480,000, figured as follows:

| Adjusted basis of contributed property | $800,000 |
|---|---|
| Minus: Part of mortgage assumed by other partners (80% × $400,000) | $320,000 |
| Basis of Karen's partnership interest | $480,000 |

If contributed property is encumbered by a liability or if a partner's liabilities are assumed by the partnership, the basis of the contributing partner's interest is reduced (but not below zero) by the liability assumed by the other partners. This partner must reduce his basis because the assumption of the liability is treated as a distribution of money to that partner. The other partners' assumption of the liability is treated as a contribution by them of money to the partnership. For more information, see **Publication 541,** *Partnerships.*

**32. The answer is D.** The corporation's charitable contribution is limited to $40,000 and figured as follows: ($600,000 - $200,000) X 10% = $40,000. A C Corporation can claim a limited deduction for charitable contributions. The deduction is limited to 10% of taxable income, calculated *before* the charitable contribution, Dividends Received Deduction, and net operating loss or capital loss *carrybacks.* For more information, see **Publication 542**, *Corporations.*

**33. The answer is B.** If a taxpayer trades property and also pays money, the basis of the property received is the basis of the property given up, increased by any additional money paid. In a non-taxable property exchange, the additional money is also called "boot." The answer is figured as follows:

| | |
|---|---|
| Cost of old equipment | $50,000 |
| MINUS Depreciation on old equipment | $26,000 |
| Adjusted basis old equipment | $24,000 |
| ADD Cash paid (boot) for new equipment | $12,000 |
| Adjusted basis new equipment | $36,000 |

**34. The answer is C.** A qualified Personal Service Corporation is taxed at a flat rate of 35% on taxable income. A Personal Service Corporation is a corporation where:

- The main work of the company is to perform services in the fields of health (including veterinary services), law, engineering, architecture, accounting, actuarial science, the performing arts, or consulting.
- Substantially all of the stock is owned by employees, retired employees, or their estates.

Examples include law firms and medical clinics. For more information, see **Publication 542**, *Corporations.*

**35. The answer is B.** Corporations generally must make estimated tax payments if they expect their estimated tax (income tax less credits) to be $500 or more. For more information, see **Instructions for Form 1120**.

**36. The answer is A.** Because ABC Corporation has over 80% ownership of DDD Corporation, the dividends are not taxable. ABC Corporation may claim the Dividends Received Deduction for the dividends received from DDD Corporation.

**37. The answer is D.** None of the vehicles listed is considered listed property. A vehicle used in a business of transporting persons (such as a tour bus or ambulance) or property for hire (such as a taxi cab) is not listed property. The following vehicles are NOT considered listed property:

- An ambulance or hearse
- A vehicle used directly in the trade or business of transporting persons or property for pay or hire, such as a taxi, shuttle, or other similar vehicles
- A truck or van that is a qualified non-personal use vehicle, such as a furniture delivery van that is only used for furniture delivery at a business location

For more information, see **Publication 946,** *How to Depreciate Property.*

**38. The answer is D.** Livestock is eligible for the Section 179 deduction. The other assets listed do not qualify for any type of accelerated depreciation. For more information, see **Publication 946,** *How to Depreciate Property.*

**39. The answer is D.** A stock distribution is generally not a taxable event. In a stock distribution, a corporation is not actually distributing money (which would then be taxable); instead, it distributes shares of its own stock. Distributions by a corporation of its own stock are also commonly known as "stock dividends" or "stock rights." Stock rights are distributions by a corporation of "rights" to acquire the corporation's stock. Generally, stock dividends and stock rights are not taxable to shareholders and not deductible by the corporation.

**40. The answer is B.** The ordinary income is figured as follows ($50,000 - $20,000 in expenses). The tax-exempt interest and rental income is separately stated income, and the charitable contributions are separately stated items. The charitable contributions deduction is taken by the individual shareholder on his individual return.

**41. The answer is B.** Contributions to a partner's retirement account are treated as a distribution to the partner. The amount is a separately stated item on **Form 1065.**

**42. The answer is C.** A C Corporation is not a pass-through entity. There are many benefits to incorporation. However, one of the main drawbacks of a C Corporation is the tax ramifications of this entity type. Unlike a partnership, a sole proprietorship, or an S Corporation, the earnings of a C Corporation are taxed twice. Corporate income is taxed when it is earned and then taxed again when it is distributed to shareholders as dividends. A corporation does not receive a tax deduction for the distribution of dividends to its shareholders.

**43. The answer is A.** If a corporation cancels a shareholder's debt without repayment by the shareholder, the amount canceled is treated as a distribution to the shareholder. A corporate distribution to a shareholder is generally treated as a distribution of earnings and profits.

**44. The answer is A.** Gracie Corp. must recognize a taxable gain of $60,000. This transaction is treated as a sale. It is as if Gracie Corp. sold the building for $250,000 and used the profits from the sale to pay the debt. Gracie must realize a taxable gain as if the property had been sold at its fair market value and the proceeds were used to pay off the creditor. This is the correct treatment when a taxpayer repays a debt with appreciated property.

**45. The answer is D.** A Personal Service Corporation pays corporate tax at a flat rate of 35%. The answer is figured as follows: ($68,000 - $22,000 NOL) X 35% = $16,100.

**46. The answer is A.** In this case, Gabe is considered to have 100% of constructive ownership in the partnership, because the rules for "constructive ownership" include the ownership of his family. For this rule, "family" includes ONLY brothers, sisters, spouses, ancestors, and lineal descendants. Therefore, the ownership is figured as follows:

| | |
|---|---|
| Gabe | 20% |
| Gabe's son | 20% |
| Gabe's brother | 60% |
| Ownership | 100% |

For more information, see **Publication 550**, *Investment Income and Expenses*.

**47. The answer is B.** A corporation's treatment of distributions is different during a complete liquidation. In a liquidation, a corporation recognizes gain on appreciated assets and losses on depreciated property. Shareholders also recognize gain or loss on a corporation's distribution of assets during a liquidation. In this case, Gordon's gain would be figured as follows:

$10,000 + $12,000 = $22,000 distribution

$22,000 - $17,000 stock basis = $5,000 gain

Corporate liquidations of property generally are treated as a sale or exchange. Gain or loss generally is recognized by the corporation on a liquidating **sale** of its assets. Gain or loss generally is *also* recognized on a liquidating **distribution** of assets as if the corporation sold the assets to the distributee at fair market value. To find out more, refer to **Publication 544,** *Sales and Other Dispositions of Assets.*

**48. The answer is A.** The IRS may reclassify the excess $1,500 per month in rental payments as a constructive dividend, and the corporation would lose that amount as a deduction. If a corporation rents property from a shareholder and the rent is unreasonably more than the shareholder would charge to a stranger to rent the same property, the excessive part of the rent may be treated as a distribution to the shareholder. For more information, see **Publication 542**, *Corporations.*

**49. The answer is B.** If a corporation issues bonds and then later repurchases the bonds at a higher price than the original issue price, then the corporation has a deduction for interest expense in the year of the repurchase. Therefore, the corporation should report an interest expense of $30,000 ($580,000 - $550,000), IRC Section 1.163-4.

**50. The answer is B.** A married couple who jointly operate a business may choose for each spouse to be treated as a sole proprietor by electing to file as a "qualified joint venture." Unless a business meets the requirements of a qualified joint venture, a sole proprietorship must be solely owned by one spouse and the other spouse may work in the business as an employee. A business jointly owned and operated by a husband and wife is generally treated as a partnership unless the spouses elect to be treated as a qualified joint venture. For more information, see **Publication 334,** *Tax Guide for Small Business.*

**51. The answer is C.** A gain of $70,000 = ($160,000 – $90,000) must be recognized, because only $80,000 was reinvested. If property is condemned (or disposed of under the threat of condemnation), figure gain or loss by comparing the adjusted basis of the condemned property with the net condemnation award. For more information, see **Publication 544**, *Sales and Other Dispositions of Assets.*

**52. The answer is A.** Earned income, including wages that are paid to the taxpayer's own children, are NOT subject to the "kiddie tax," regardless of the child's age. Wages of a child under age 18 who works for his parent in a business are not subject to Social Security and Medicare taxes if the trade or business is a sole proprietorship or a partnership in which each partner is a parent of the child. Payments for the services of a child of any age who works for his parent are generally subject to income tax withholding. For more information, see **Publication 15,** *(Circular E), Employer's Tax Guide.*

**53. The answer is D.** Since XYZ is an accrual-basis corporation, the wages are deductible as they are accrued. The full amount of the bonus and other wages to the other employees is deductible in 2011.

**54. The answer is D.** Tips are considered taxable income and are subject to federal income taxes. Tips that an employee receives from customers are generally subject to withholding. Employees must report tips they receive to their employer by the tenth of the month after the month that the tips are received. Employers are required to collect income tax, employee Social Security tax, and employee Medicare tax on the employee's tips. For more information on the taxation of tips, see **Publication 15,** *(Circular E), Employer's Tax Guide.*

**55. The answer is A.** C Corporations report income and loss on **Form 1120**, *U.S. Corporation Income Tax Return.*

**56. The answer is B.** An LLC can file Form 8832 to elect its business entity classification. A business with at least two members can choose to be classified as a corporation or a partnership, and a business entity with a single member can choose to be classified as either a corporation or disregarded as an entity separate from its owner (a "disregarded entity").

**57. The answer is B.** An interest in a partnership or joint venture is treated as a capital asset when it is sold. However, any gain or loss from unrealized receivables or inventory items will be treated as ordinary gain or loss. For more information, see **Publication 541,** *Partnerships.*

**58. The answer is B.** If a partnership's debt is canceled because of bankruptcy or insolvency, the rules for the exclusion of the canceled amount from gross income and for tax attribute reduction are applied at the **individual partner level**. Thus, each partner's share of debt cancellation income must be reported on the partner's individual tax return. The allocation of debt cancellation income to a partner results in that partner's basis in the partnership being *increased* by that amount. At the same time, the reduction in the partner's share of partnership liabilities caused by the debt cancellation results in a deemed distribution, in turn resulting in a reduction of the partner's basis in the partnership. For more information, see **Publication 908**, *Bankruptcy Tax Guide*.

**59. The answer is C.** The corporation's *unextended* due date is September 15, 2011, so the six-month corporate extension to file makes the NEW due date March 15, 2012.

**60. The answer is C.** The answer is figured as follows:

($190,000 - $35,000) = $155,000

($155,000 X 39%) = $60,450

The capital loss can only offset capital gain. Therefore, the capital loss cannot be currently deducted and must be carried over to a future year.

**61. The answer is C.** Ned must reduce the basis of his stock. A non-dividend distribution is a distribution that is not paid out of the earnings and profits of a corporation. A non-dividend distribution reduces the basis of the shareholder's stock. It is not taxed until the basis in the stock is fully recovered. This non-taxable portion is also called a return of capital. It is a return of Ned's investment in the stock of the company. When the basis of the stock has been reduced to zero, any additional non-dividend distribution that is received must be reported as a capital gain.

**62. The answer is C. Form 990-T** is currently used by tax-exempt organizations to report and pay the tax on unrelated business income. **Form 990-T**, *Exempt Organization Business Income Tax Return*, is used by a tax exempt entity to:

- Report unrelated business income;
- Claim a refund of income tax paid by a Regulated Investment Company (RIC) or a Real Estate Investment Trust (REIT) on undistributed long-term capital gain; and
- Request a credit for certain federal excise taxes paid.

Any domestic or foreign tax-exempt organization must file **Form 990-T** if it has gross income from an unrelated trade or business of $1,000 or more.

**63. The answer is A.** Renee must reduce her basis in the partnership interest to zero. She will have a $32,000 basis in the land. A partner cannot have a negative partnership basis. She does not recognize any income in this transaction. Renee will defer any gain on the land until she sells it. If Renee had received cash instead of property, she would have been forced to recognize the gain.

**64. The answer is B.** The video recorder, laptop, and digital camera are all considered listed property. The Small Business Jobs and Credit Act of 2010 removed cellular telephones from the category of listed property.

| Video recorder | $195 |
|---|---|
| Laptop | $450 |
| Digital camera | $123 |
| **Total** | **$768** |

The following property is considered *listed property* by the IRS:

- Passenger automobiles weighing 6,000 pounds or less.
- Any other property used for transportation, unless it is an excepted vehicle. Certain vehicles are not considered listed property; these include examples like ambulances, police cars, hearses, taxis, moving vans, or any other vehicles that are qualified as "non-personal use." These include trucks and vans that have been modified so that they are not used for personal purposes, such as by installation of permanent shelving and painting the vehicles to display advertising or the company's name.
- Property generally used for entertainment, recreation, or amusement (including photographic, phonographic, communication, and video-recording equipment).

- Computers and related peripheral equipment, unless used only at a regular business establishment and owned or leased by the person operating the establishment.

See IRS **Publication 946,** *How to Depreciate Property,* to read more about the *listed property* rules.

**65. The answer is A.** State incorporation fees are considered qualifying organizational costs. However, the following items are capital expenses that cannot be amortized:

- Costs for issuing and selling stock or securities, such as commissions, professional fees, and printing costs.
- Costs associated with the transfer of assets to the corporation.

For more information, see **Publication 535,** *Business Expenses.*

**66. The answer is D.** In general, a business can deduct only 50% of business-related meal and entertainment expenses. However, there are some examples where meals are not subject to this limit. The following meals are NOT subject to the 50% limit:

- Meals that are included in employees' wages as taxable compensation
- Meals that qualify as a *de minimis* fringe benefit, such as occasional coffee and doughnuts
- Meals furnished to employees when the employer operates a restaurant or catering service
- Meals furnished to employees as part of a teambuilding activity, such as a company picnic
- Meals that are required by federal law to be furnished to crew members of certain commercial vessels
- Meals furnished on an oil or gas platform or drilling rig located offshore or in Alaska

These meals are 100% deductible by the employer. For more information, see **Publication 463**, *Travel, Entertainment, Gift, and Car Expenses.*

**67. The answer is A.** Since Jacob received a $10,000 cash distribution when his basis was only $7,000, he must recognize gain of $3,000 and reduce his partnership basis to zero. His partnership basis is therefore zero, and his basis on the distributed property is also zero. A partner cannot have a "negative basis." Gain is not recognized in a partnership distribution unless the distribution exceeds the partner's basis in his partnership interest. A partnership also generally does not recognize any gain or loss because of distributions made to its partners. A partner generally recognizes gain on a partnership distribution only to the extent any money distributed exceeds the adjusted basis of the partner's interest. Any gain recognized is treated as capital gain. If partnership property (in this case, Jacob got a car) is distributed to a partner, he does not recognize any gain until the sale of the property.

**68. The answer is B.** When a partnership ceases all operations, it is called a partnership liquidation. When a partnership liquidates, all the following events are deemed to occur at the same time:

- All partnership liabilities become payable in full.
- All of the partnership's assets have a value of zero (except for property contributed to secure a liability).
- All property is disposed of by the partnership in a fully taxable transaction for no consideration except relief from liabilities for which the creditor's right to reimbursement is limited solely to one or more assets of the partnership.
- All items of income, gain, loss, or deduction are allocated to the partners.
- The partnership then liquidates.

**69. The answer is D.** All of the costs must be added to the basis of the land. The original basis of an asset includes:

- The purchase price, including any borrowed money to pay for the property
- Expenses of making the purchase, such as legal fees or realtor fees
- Any existing liabilities that the seller assumes (such as delinquent property taxes)

Any demolition costs are added to the basis of the land. Other related costs incurred for the demolition of any building are added to the basis of the land on which the demolished building was located. The costs cannot be claimed as a current deduction. For more information, see **Publication 551,** *Basis of Assets.*

**70. The answer is C.** Lynden Corp. must include the $12,000 on each employee's **Form W-2** because it is taxable as wages. The amounts are subject to withholding, as well as to Social Security and Medicare tax. The car allowance is treated as part of a non-accountable plan. For more information, see **Publication 463,** *Travel, Entertainment, Gift, and Car Expenses.*

**71. The answer is A.** The death of a partner closes the partnership's tax year for that partner. Generally, it does not close the partnership's tax year for the remaining partners. The decedent's distributive share of partnership items must be figured as if the partnership's tax year ended on the date the partner died.

**72. The answer is B.** Software development in the United States qualifies for the Domestic Production Activities Deduction. Only certain activities qualify for the DPAD. The deduction applies to activities related to installing, developing, improving, or creating goods that are "manufactured, produced, or grown within the United States." This deduction also applies to the construction of real property in the United States, domestic software development, and any qualified domestic film production (except for pornographic films.) The following types of business are specifically excluded from claiming the DPAD:

- Construction services that are cosmetic in nature, such as drywall and painting
- Leasing or licensing items to a related party
- Selling food or beverages prepared at restaurants or dining establishments
- The transmission or distribution of electricity, natural gas, or water
- Any advertising, product placement, customer service businesses, and other telecommunications services

The deduction is claimed on **Form 8903.**

**73. The answer is A.** *Depletion* is the "using up" of natural resources by mining, quarrying, drilling, or felling. The Depletion Deduction allows an owner to account for the reduction of a product's reserves. The industries that qualify for the Depletion Deduction are:

- Mining
- Timber
- Oil and gas
- Geothermal energy producers
- Other similar industries

A patent does not qualify for a Depletion Deduction because it is not a resource that gets used up. Instead, a patent would be amortized over its useful life.

**74. The answer is D.** The production of inventory is subject to the Uniform Capitalization Rules (UCR). Under the UCR, businesses must capitalize the direct costs for production of goods. In most cases, the UCR also applies to businesses that purchase merchandise for resale to others. In essence, the UCR rules affect almost any business that carries or produces inventory. The Uniform Capitalization Rules do NOT apply to the following:

- Resellers of personal property with average annual gross receipts of $10 million or less for the three prior tax years
- Non-business property (such as a hobby that is not operated for profit, but produces occasional income)
- Research and experimental expenditures
- Intangible drilling and development costs of oil and gas or geothermal wells
- Property produced under a long-term contract
- Timber raised, harvested, or grown, and the underlying land
- Qualified creative expenses incurred as freelance (self-employed) writers, photographers, or artists that are otherwise deductible on their tax returns
- Loan originations

**75. The answer is B.** An estate tax return is filed on **Form 706**, *United States Estate (and Generation-Skipping Transfer) Tax Return.*

**76. The answer is A.** Chris realizes $25,000 from the sale of his partnership interest ($10,000 cash payment + $15,000 liability relief). He reports $4,000 ($25,000 realized – $21,000 basis) as a capital gain. The sale of a partner's interest in a partnership usually results in capital gain or loss. Gain (or loss) is the difference between the amount realized and the adjusted basis of the partner's interest in the partnership. If the selling partner is relieved of any partnership liabilities, that partner must include the liability relief as part of the amount realized. See IRS **Publication 541,** *Partnerships.*

**77. The answer is A.** Diamondback's taxable income is $80,000 ($100,000 dividends - $20,000 NOL). The tentative Dividends Received Deduction will not cause a net operating loss, so the Dividends Received Deduction is limited to 70% of Diamondback's taxable income. The problem is figured as follows:

($100,000 dividends - $20,000 NOL) = $80,000 income (before the Dividends Received Deduction)
$80,000 X 70% = $56,000

**78. The answer is A.** The cost of defending or perfecting a title *increases* an asset's basis. The following table shows common increases and decreases to basis:

| Increases to Basis | Decreases to Basis |
|---|---|
| Putting an addition on a home | Non-taxable corporate distributions |
| Replacing an entire roof | Casualty or theft loss deductions and subsequent insurance reimbursements |
| Installing central air conditioning | Credit for qualified electric vehicles |
| Rewiring a rental property | Section 179 deduction |
| Assessments for local improvements | Deduction for clean-fuel vehicles and clean-fuel vehicle refueling property |
| Water connections, sidewalks, roads | Depreciation |
| Casualty losses (and subsequent repairs without insurance reimbursement) | Depletion |
| Restoring damaged property | Amortization |
| Legal fees | Rebates from a manufacturer |

For more information, see **Publication 551**, *Basis of Assets.*

**79. The answer is A.** A trust must file IRS **Form 1041** in order to report income, loss, and distributions. The fiduciary fee is deductible in arriving at taxable income, and the fiduciary fee must be allocated between taxable and non-taxable income. The answer is figured as follows: ($4,000 - $500 fiduciary fee) = $3,500 in taxable income to be distributed.

**80. The answer is C.** A church is not required to file an information return to report its income and loss. This is the exception to the rule. Most exempt organizations are required to file **Form 990**. Churches are also exempted by law from payment of federal income tax and therefore they are not required to file an application for exemption with the IRS, but many churches still do seek formal exemption. Federal law imposes several reporting requirements on charitable organizations, but the main reporting requirements for churches have to do with employment taxes (when they pay employees) and Unrelated Business Income Tax, or UBIT. An exempt organization that has $1,000 or more of gross income from an unrelated business must file **Form 990–T**. Since Trinity does not have $1,000 of UBIT, it is not required to file **Form 990-T**, but it is still required to file employment tax returns (the **Form 941** series), because it pays employee wages.

**81. The answer is B.** In order to apply for recognition of exempt status by the IRS under Section 501(c)(3) of the IRC, entities use Form 1023, *Application for Recognition of Exemption*. Tax-exempt organizations are organized primarily for religious, charitable, scientific, educational, or literary purposes. Organizations created to prevent cruelty to animals or children also qualify. There are two forms used by non-profit organizations to request exemption. Organizations that *do not qualify* for exemption under Section 501(c)(3) may still qualify for tax-exempt status under another code section. They can file Form 1024, *Application for Recognition of Exemption Under 501(a)*. Read more about exempt entities and their filing requirements in Book 2 of your PassKey study guide, or read IRS **Publication 557**.

**82. The answer is B.** The exchange of partnership interests is NOT a qualifying 1031 exchange. Certain property does NOT qualify for Section 1031 exchange treatment. Section 1031 does NOT apply to exchanges of:

- Inventory
- Stocks, bonds, notes, or other securities
- Livestock of different sexes
- Real property in the United States and real property outside the United States
- Shares of corporate stock in different companies
- Partnership interests in different partnerships

A 1031 exchange applies to business property or property held for investment only. The rules regarding like-kind exchanges are VERY STRICT. Internal Revenue Code Section 1031 says that owners may defer gain on the disposal of business property if they exchange it for another item of business property of a similar type (i.e., residential rental for an apartment building). The tax liability is not eliminated; it is simply *deferred* until the eventual sale or disposal of the newly acquired item. To qualify for a non-taxable 1031 exchange:

- The property must be business or investment property.
- The property must not be property held for sale (such as inventory, acquired specifically for resale).
- There must be an actual exchange of property.
- Tangible personal property can be either "like-kind" or "like-class."
- Intangible personal property must be "like-kind."
- The transferor must identify the property to be received within 45 days after the date the original property is given up in the exchange.
- The exchange must be completed within 180 days.

**83. The answer is A.** Section 1245 property does not include buildings and their structural components. Section 1245 deals with gains from the disposition of property on which depreciation had been previously claimed. Generally, the gains on Section 1245 property are taxed at the capital gains rate except to the extent of depreciation claimed, which is taxed as ordinary income.

**84. The answer is C.** Leisure Corp. will recognize neither gain nor loss on the sale of the asset. There is no loss recognized in this transaction because this is a sale to a related party. A loss on the sale of an asset to a related party is not allowed unless the distribution is done in a complete liquidation. The rules for "related party" transactions are complex and important to understand for Part 2 of the EA exam. In this case, "related parties" include members of a family, including brothers and sisters, spouse, ancestors (e.g., parents, grandparents), and lineal descendants (children, grandchildren). This list is not exhaustive, and related parties can also be entities. IRC Section 267 not only applies to family members, but also includes related businesses, trusts, fiduciaries, and a host of other transactions. Take the time to review the related party transaction rules in your study guide.

**85. The answer is D.** An accrual-based C Corporation is allowed to deduct charitable contributions authorized during the taxable year by the board of directors and paid by the 15th day of the third month following the close of the taxable year.

**86. The answer is B.** In general, a taxpayer has two years after the year that the involuntary conversion occurred to replace the property and make the reinvestment. However, there are special rules for certain types of property. For real estate, the replacement period is generally three years after the close of the year in which the gain is realized. If the involuntary conversion property is not replaced within the allowed time period, an amended tax return would have to be filed, claiming the income as taxable.

**87. The answer is A.** Kristy will be forced to recognize $2,800 in imputed interest as dividend income. When a corporation makes an interest-free loan or a below-market loan to a shareholder, the imputed interest is deemed to be a taxable dividend. The corporation is not allowed to take a deduction for the imputed dividends that were paid. However, if the loan is made to an employee, the treatment of the imputed interest is different. When an employer makes an interest-free loan or a below-market loan to an employee, then the imputed interest is considered taxable compensation to the employee and is deductible by the employer. For more information, see **Publication 542**, *Corporations.*

**88. The answer is B.** In 2011, Congress decreased the amount allowed as a deduction for startup expenditures to $5,000. If startup expenses exceed $50,000, there is a dollar for dollar reduction until the deduction is eliminated. The deduction for organizational costs remained the same at $5,000 with a phase-out range of $50,000. Any remaining costs must be amortized over 180 months (15 years).

**89. The answer is D.** Prepayment penalties on a mortgage are deductible as interest expense. The other items listed cannot be taken as business expenses. Any type of political contribution, kickbacks, or any cost that is incurred to try to influence legislation is not deductible as a business expense. Repairs to equipment that add value to the asset or increase its useful life are considered improvements and must be capitalized and depreciated.

**90. The answer is C.** The original basis, which is $140,000 ($30,000 + $110,000), must be reduced by the depreciation. Therefore, Sam's adjusted basis in the building before the sale is $118,000 ($140,000 - $22,000). The gain is then figured as follows: ($205,000 - $118,000 basis) = $87,000 gain. The gain is allocated as follows: $22,000 of the $87,000 gain will be recognized as ordinary income (depreciation recapture) and the remaining $65,000 would be taxed as a capital gain.

**91. The answer is D.** An exempt entity may file a request for exemption within 15 months of initial organization. Retroactive exemption is still available within that time period.

**92. The answer is B.** The answer is figured as follows:

| Gross receipts | $42,000 |
|---|---|
| Supplies expense | ($3,500) |
| Wages for part-time employee | ($5,000) |
| Utility expenses | ($800) |
| Income | $32,700 |

The amounts for the Section 1231 gain and the charitable contributions are not reported on **Schedule C**. Section 1231 gains and losses are netted against each other in the same manner as capital gains and losses (for example, the gains and losses from a stock sale), except that a Section 1231 gain is considered a capital gain, while a Section 1231 loss is treated as an ordinary loss for tax purposes. For more information, see **Publication 544**, *Sales and Other Dispositions of Assets.*

**93. The answer is C.** In spite of having received only a $23,000 distribution, Angie must include $27,000 = (30% X $90,000) in her gross income for the year. A partner pays tax on income that is earned, even if it is not distributed. In spite of having received only a $23,000 distribution, Angie must include $27,000 = (30% X

$90,000) in her gross income for the year. Partnership income earned by a general partner is considered income from self-employment and is subject to self-employment tax.

**94. The answer is A.** An S Corporation is a pass-through entity. An eligible domestic corporation can avoid double taxation (once to the shareholders and again to the corporation) by electing to be treated as an S Corporation. In this respect, an S Corporation is taxed more like a partnership.

**95. The answer is D.** Itemized deductions are only available on individual tax returns.

**96. The answer is B.** The answer is figured as follows:

$120,000 X 80% = $96,000 Dividends Received Deduction

A corporation can deduct a percentage of certain dividends received during its tax year. This is called the "Dividends Received Deduction." The Dividends Received Deduction is a tax deduction received by a corporation on the dividends paid to it by other corporations in which it has an ownership stake. If the corporation receiving the dividend owns 20% of the other corporation, then the deduction is 80%. *Note: Be very careful when you read these questions on the EA exam. Sometimes the question will ask for the corporation's taxable income, rather than the deduction amount.

**97. The answer is A.** Since Temple Corporation is on a fiscal tax year ending June 30, then its payments are due on October 15, December 15, March 15, and June 15. Installment payments for estimated tax are due by the fifteenth day of the fourth, sixth, ninth, and twelfth months of the corporation's tax year. If a corporation is on a calendar year, then its tax year ends December 31. Installment payments are due on April 15, June 15, September 15, and December 15. If any due date falls on a Saturday, Sunday, or legal holiday, the installment is due on the next business day.

**98. The answer is C.** The corporation treats this $6,000 as a short-term loss that must be **carried back for three years** and **carried forward for up to five years**. When a corporation carries a net capital loss to another tax year, it's treated as a short-term loss. It does not retain its original identity as long-term or short-term. A corporation can deduct capital losses only up to the amount of its capital gains. In other words, if a corporation has an excess capital loss, it cannot deduct the loss in the current tax year. A capital loss is carried to other years in the following order:

- Three years prior to the loss year
- Two years prior to the loss year
- One year prior to the loss year

Any loss remaining is carried forward for five years. Capital losses incurred by a C Corporation can only be used to offset capital gains, not ordinary income. There is no "$3,000 allowance" for corporations. The "$3,000 allowance" for capital losses to offset ordinary income only applies to individual taxpayers.

**99. The answer is C.** The Section 179 Deduction limit was unchanged in 2011. The total amount of qualifying property that can be purchased is $2 million, before the deduction is subject to a phase-out. Section 179 includes most new and used equipment. There is a special rule that allows taxpayers to deduct up to $250,000 of Qualified Real Property (QRP) under Section 179. The taxpayer must elect to treat QRP as Section 179 property. This special provision only applies to certain industries and property types[5] and includes the following real property:

- Qualified leasehold improvement property
- Qualified restaurant property (improvements to a restaurant building, such as a major renovation)
- Qualified retail improvement property (for example, an improvement of a retail clothing store, including major interior upgrades and other similar improvements)

The maximum amount of Section 179 expenses for QRP is limited to $250,000 (although a business is still eligible to deduct the full $500,000 limit for other qualifying property).

---

[5] Included in the Small Business Jobs Act of 2010

**100. The answer is C.** An S-election may be revoked if shareholders holding more than 50% of the stock agree to the termination. Since Charlotte and Thomas own more than 50% of the outstanding stock, they can elect to revoke the S-election.

# Representation: Answers

**1. The answer is A.** Tania is not a tax return preparer and is not required to have a PTIN. New regulations require all paid tax return preparers (including attorneys, CPAs, and Enrolled Agents) to apply for a Preparer Tax Identification Number (PTIN). Employees are also bound by this new requirement, but only if the employee prepares tax returns. Employees that simply offer technical or office help are not required to obtain a PTIN.

**2. The answer is B.** Tax returns prepared by a paid preparer but filed on paper must be submitted with **Form 8948**, *Preparer Explanation for Not Filing Electronically.* A reason must be provided for each return that is not e-filed.

**3. The answer is A.** A Registered Tax Return Preparer may represent a taxpayer only on issues related to the tax return he prepared for that same taxpayer. If providing representation services, the Registered Tax Return Preparer may only represent the taxpayer before the IRS examination function. For more information, see **Publication 470**, *Limited Practice Without Enrollment*.

**4. The answer is B.** The "enrollment cycle" refers to the three successive enrollment years preceding the effective date of renewal.

**5. The answer is E.** All of the practitioners listed above qualify to represent a taxpayer before the IRS, under certain circumstances. Student volunteers at a VITA site are given a special exemption to represent taxpayers before the IRS. VITA is the IRS's volunteer income tax preparation program, designed specifically to help low income taxpayers. For more information, see **Circular 230**.

**6. The answer is B.** There are special restrictions on EIC claims by taxpayers that have had previous EIC claims denied. A taxpayer who was determined to have claimed the EIC due to reckless or intentional disregard of the EIC rules cannot claim the EIC for two tax years. If the error was due to outright fraud, then the taxpayer cannot claim the EIC for ten tax years. For more information, see **Publication 596,** *Earned Income Credit*.

**7. The answer is B.** Records must be kept for a period of three years. Individuals applying for renewal of enrollment must retain CPE records for three years following the date of renewal. Program *sponsors* must maintain records to verify the participants who attended and completed the program for a period of three years following completion of the program.

**8. The answer is B.** Randall needs a PTIN, but he does not need to pass a competency test. All paid preparers need a PTIN. However, certain "supervised preparers" do not need to pass a competency test if they are employed by a law firm, CPA firm, or other tax firm (a firm that is at least 80% owned by attorneys, CPAs, or Enrolled Agents), provided the returns prepared are signed by an attorney, CPA, or an Enrolled Agent who is employed by the same firm and has a valid PTIN. Additional guidance on "supervised preparers" is available in IRS Notice 2011-6.

**9. The answer is A. Form 23** is the application for enrollment. Applicants must undergo a background check prior to enrollment. It takes about 120 days to be issued an enrollment card.

**10. The answer is A. Form 8857** is used to request innocent spouse relief. Innocent spouse relief provides relief from additional tax owed if a spouse or former spouse failed to report income, reported income improperly, or claimed improper deductions or credits. See **Publication 971** for more information on innocent spouse relief.

**11. The answer is D.** Doug may use the phrase, *"Enrolled to practice before the Internal Revenue Service."* Enrolled Agents, in describing their professional designation, may not use the term "certified" or imply any type of employment relationship with the IRS. Examples of acceptable descriptions for Enrolled Agents are "enrolled to represent taxpayers before the Internal Revenue Service," "enrolled to practice before the Internal Revenue Service," and "admitted to practice before the Internal Revenue Service." For more information, see **Circular 230**.

**12. The answer is D.** A PTIN cannot be shared. A PTIN is an individual preparer's number. Each preparer must obtain his or her own PTIN.

**13. The answer is A.** Practitioners may not use official IRS insignia in their advertising. A practitioner *may* use the IRS e-file logo. A preparer may NOT combine the e-file logo with the IRS eagle symbol, the word "federal," or with other words or symbols that suggest a special relationship between the IRS and the practitioner. Advertising materials must not carry the FMS (The IRS Financial Management Service), IRS, or other Treasury seals. For more information, see **Circular 230**.

**Allowed:**

**Prohibited:**

**14. The answer is D.** Alimony is not considered qualifying income for the purpose of the EIC. Qualifying earned income includes:

- Wages, salaries, and tips.
- Union strike benefits.
- Long-term disability benefits received prior to minimum retirement age.
- Net earnings from self-employment.
- *Combat Pay: A taxpayer can *elect* to have non-taxable combat pay included in earned income for the Earned Income Credit.

**15. The answer is D.** A levy does not apply to the taxpayer's clothing and undelivered mail. Property exempt from levy includes the following:

- Clothing and school books necessary for the taxpayer and family.
- Judgments for support of minor children (as well as other limited types of income).
- Certain service-connected disability payments.
- Fuel, provisions, furniture, and personal effects not exceeding $6,250.
- Books and tools necessary for the taxpayer's trade not exceeding $3,125 in value.
- Undelivered mail.
- The taxpayer's principal residence (usually). After 1998, the seizure of a personal residence by the IRS is prohibited for any liability under $5,000. For all liabilities of $5,000 or more, the IRS must obtain approval from a U.S. District Court judge or magistrate prior to seizing a personal residence. (IRC §6334).

An IRS levy refers to the actual seizing of property authorized by a tax lien, so it is a legal seizure of property. A tax lien, on the other hand, is the IRS's *authorization* to act.

**16. The answer is A.** To claim the EIC, the taxpayer (and spouse, if filing a joint return) must have a valid SSN issued by the Social Security Administration. Any qualifying child listed on Schedule EIC also must have a valid SSN.

**17. The answer is D.** A practitioner may NOT charge a contingent fee (percentage of the refund) for preparing an original tax return. Separate fees may NOT be charged for Direct Deposits, and e-file providers are still required to sign an e-filed return with an electronic signature (Circular 230).

**18. The answer is A.** Simply preparing a tax return, furnishing information at the request of the IRS, or appearing as a witness for the taxpayer is not practice before the IRS. These acts can be performed by anyone. Practice before the IRS covers all matters relating to any of the following:

- Communicating with the IRS on behalf of a taxpayer regarding the taxpayer's rights, privileges, or liabilities under laws and regulations administered by the IRS.
- Representing a taxpayer at conferences, hearings, or meetings with the IRS.
- Preparing and filing documents with the IRS for a taxpayer.
- Corresponding and communicating on behalf of a taxpayer.

For more information, see **Circular 230**.

**19. The answer is D.** Applicants for renewal of enrollment must file Form 8554, *Application for Renewal of Enrollment to Practice Before the Internal Revenue Service.* To qualify for renewal, applicants must complete the necessary hours of continuing professional education during each three-year enrollment cycle. For more information, see **Circular 230**.

**20. The answer is D.** Receipt of taxpayer refund checks is allowed, but the tax practitioner must have a power of attorney in order to do so. A tax practitioner may never cash (or endorse) a taxpayer refund check. A power of attorney is not required in some situations when dealing with the IRS. The following situations do not require a power of attorney:

- Providing information to the IRS
- Authorizing the disclosure of tax return information through Form 8821
- Allowing the IRS to discuss return information with a third party designee
- Allowing a tax matters partner or person (TMP) to perform acts for the partnership
- Allowing the IRS to discuss return information with a fiduciary
- Representing a taxpayer through a non-written consent

These exceptions are discussed in detail in IRS **Publication 947**.

**21. The answer is B.** A third-party designee may respond to IRS notices about math errors, offsets, and return preparation. The taxpayer completes the Third Party Designee Authorization directly on the tax return, entering the designee's name and phone number and a self-selected five-digit PIN, which the designee will have to confirm when requesting information from the IRS. A third party designee may:

- Exchange information concerning the return with the IRS;
- Call the IRS for information about the processing of the return or the status of refund or payments;
- Request and receive written tax return information relating to the tax return, including copies of notices, correspondence, and account transcripts; and
- Respond to certain IRS notices about math errors, offsets, and return preparation.

The taxpayer is not authorizing the designee to receive any refund check, bind the taxpayer to any IRS contract or agreement (including additional tax liability), or otherwise represent the taxpayer before the IRS.

**22. The answer is D.** The IRS may accept an Offer in Compromise based on *three* grounds: (a) doubt as to collectability, (b) effective tax administration, and (c) doubt as to liability.

**23. The answer is B.** The Internal Revenue Code (or IRC) is the main body of domestic tax law of the United States.

**24. The answer is C.** Lloyd must notify Agnes of the error and tell her the consequences of not correcting it. But he is not required to amend prior year tax returns to correct the error. A tax practitioner is *required* by **Circular 230** to advise the taxpayer when he becomes aware that the client has not complied with the revenue laws of the United States. However, the practitioner is not responsible for fixing the non-compliance issue once he has notified the client of the issue. The tax professional is also not responsible for notifying the IRS of non-compliance.

**25. The answer is A.** A tax practitioner may not charge a separate fee for Direct Deposit. Charging a flat fee for e-filing is allowed. Contingent fees for e-filing are not permitted. A practitioner may charge fees based on the following:

- Fixed fees for specific routine services
- Hourly fee rates
- Range of fees for particular services
- Fee charged for an initial consultation

**26. The answer is A.** In order to apply for an OIC, a taxpayer must submit a $150 application fee and initial payment along with **Form 656**, *Offer in Compromise*.

**27. The answer is A.** Taxpayers can now split Direct Deposits between up to three qualified accounts by using **Form 8888**, *Allocation of Refund (Including Savings Bond Purchases.*

**28. The answer is B.** Preparers who anticipate filing 11 or more **Forms 1040, 1040A, 1040EZ,** and **Forms 1041** (fiduciary returns) during the year must use IRS e-file. The requirement also applies to tax preparation firms, which must compute the number of returns prepared by its members in the aggregate. Business tax returns, such as **Form 1120** or **Form 1065**, are not subject to the current e-file mandate, (although some very large business returns do have an e-file requirement).

**29. The answer is C.** Any individual who is paid a fee to prepare a return must sign it and fill out the preparer area of the return. This is true even when the client is a family member. An employee working for an employer does not have to sign the return. Rather, the employer is the one who has the ultimate liability for the return's accuracy.

**30. The answer is D.** Tax returns bearing an ATIN may be e-filed. There are certain tax returns that cannot be e-filed. Returns with paper attachments and other odd requirements must be filed on paper. The following returns cannot be e-filed:

- Prior year tax returns;
- Tax returns with fiscal year tax periods (for business entities);
- Amended tax returns;
- Tax returns with Taxpayer Identification Numbers (TIN) within the range of 900-00-0000 through 999-99-9999. Exception: Adopted Taxpayer Identification Numbers (ATIN) and some Individual Taxpayer Identification Numbers (ITIN) may fall within the range above.

The IRS cannot electronically process tax returns with rare or unusual processing conditions or that exceed the specifications for returns allowable in IRS e-file. These conditions change from year to year. If Providers transmit electronic return data with one of these conditions, the IRS rejects the return and the taxpayer will have to file on paper.

**31. The answer is C.** A "Responsible Official" is usually the owner of the tax practice. A Responsible Official is an individual with authority over the Provider's IRS e-file operation at a location, is the first point of contact with the IRS, and has authority to sign revised IRS e-file applications. A Responsible Official ensures the Provider adheres to all rules and notices governing IRS e-file. The Responsible Official may oversee IRS e-file operations at one or more offices, but must be able to fulfill identified responsibilities for each of the offices. For more information, see **Publication 3112**, *IRS e-file Application and Participation*.

**32. The answer is B.** When an individual strikes out the jurat on a return, it becomes a "fraudulent return." The jurat is an affidavit in which the taxpayer and/or preparer attests to the truth of the information contained in the return and attached return information.

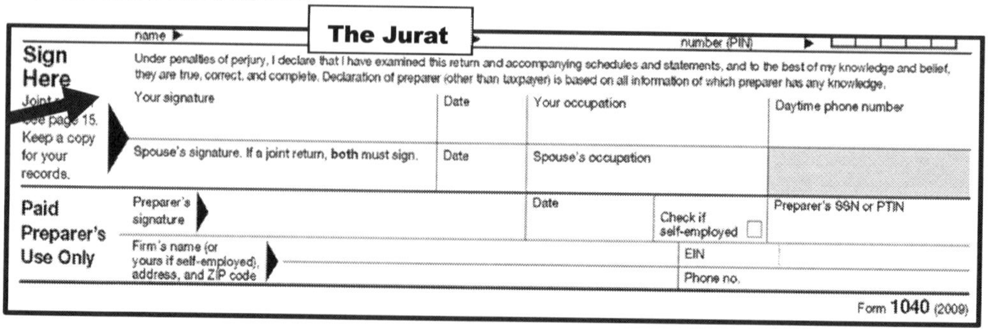
The Jurat

Sign Here
Joint return? See page 15.
Keep a copy for your records.

Under penalties of perjury, I declare that I have examined this return and accompanying schedules and statements, and to the best of my knowledge and belief, they are true, correct, and complete. Declaration of preparer (other than taxpayer) is based on all information of which preparer has any knowledge.

| Your signature | Date | Your occupation | Daytime phone number |
|---|---|---|---|
| Spouse's signature. If a joint return, **both** must sign. | Date | Spouse's occupation | |

Paid Preparer's Use Only

| Preparer's signature | Date | Check if self-employed ☐ | Preparer's SSN or PTIN |
|---|---|---|---|
| Firm's name (or yours if self-employed), address, and ZIP code | | EIN | |
| | | Phone no. | |

Form **1040** (2009)

Striking out or altering the jurat on a tax return is prohibited. Other indicators of abusive or fraudulent returns may be unsatisfactory responses to filing status questions, multiple returns with the same address, and missing or incomplete Schedules A and C income and expense documentation. Simply failing to read the instructions or filing an incorrect return may be grounds for the IRS to assess a penalty for negligence, but not for fraud.

**33. The answer is D.** A taxpayer or business is required to keep records relating to employment taxes for at least four years after the due date of the tax or the date such tax was paid, whichever is later. This includes **Form W-4, Form 941,** and copies of **Form W-2**.

**34. The answer is A.** A censure will not prevent a practitioner from practice before the IRS. Official sanctions include disbarment, suspension, censure, and reprimand. Disbarment is the permanent revocation of a practitioner's privilege to represent taxpayers before the IRS. A censure is a public reprimand. Unlike disbarment or suspension, censure does not affect an individual's eligibility to practice before the IRS. After being subject to OPR sanctions of either suspension or censure, the practitioner may be subject to conditions on his ability to practice.

**36. The answer is B.** In most cases, tax returns are audited for up to three years after filing. However, the IRS may audit for up to six years if there is substantial unreported income (25% or more income is unreported).

**37. The answer is D.** A power of attorney is valid until revoked. It may be revoked by the taxpayer or withdrawn by the representative, or it may be superseded by the filing of a new power of attorney for the same tax and tax period. For more information, see **Circular 230**.

**38. The answer is A.** Taxpayers must sign their returns under penalty of perjury. This means that the taxpayer must make a declaration that the return is true, correct, and complete.

**39. The answer is C.** Most paid preparers need both a PTIN and an EFIN. Each tax preparer needs to have his own PTIN. A Preparer Tax Identification Number (PTIN) is issued by the IRS to paid tax return preparers. It is used as the tax return preparer's identification number and, when applicable, must be placed in the Paid Preparer section of a tax return .An Electronic Filing Identification Number (EFIN) is a number issued by the IRS to individuals or firms that have been approved as authorized IRS e-file providers. EFINs are issued on a firm basis, and all preparers in a firm may be covered by a single EFIN. Preparer Tax Identification Numbers are issued to individuals. Electronic Filing Identification Numbers are issued to individuals or firms. Most preparers need both.

**40. The answer is C.** Performance as a notary is not considered disreputable conduct. An enrolled practitioner may also perform duties as a notary public. A practitioner who is a notary public and is engaged in a matter before the IRS (or has a material interest in the matter) cannot engage in any notary activities related to that matter. All of the other acts listed are considered disreputable conduct. In 2011, the OPR expanded the definition of "disreputable conduct" to include:

- Willfully failing to e-file returns electronically if they fall under the e-filing mandate, and
- Failing to include a valid PTIN on tax returns.

In previous years, paid preparers were not required to obtain a PTIN. (They could opt to use their SSN as an identifying number instead.) Preparers also were not required to e-file returns.

**41. The answer is B.** Tax practitioners may not notarize documents for the clients that they represent before the IRS. If the practitioner is a notary public and is employed as counsel, attorney, or agent in a matter before the IRS or has a material interest in the matter, he must not engage in any notary activities relative to that matter (Circular 230). Tax practitioners are allowed to charge contingent fees in rare cases, but never on an original return. A tax practitioner may represent clients with a conflict of interest so long as it is disclosed in writing to both parties and both parties agree. A tax practitioner may discuss and recommend tax shelters to a client, but the disclosure and ethics rules regarding tax shelters and tax shelter opinions are very strict.

**42. The answer is A. Form 8275**, *Disclosure Statement*, is filed by individuals, corporations, pass-through entities, and income tax return preparers to disclose a tax position on a tax return.

**43. The answer is D.** Tax preparers must not endorse or otherwise cash any refund check issued to the taxpayer. A tax preparer cannot withhold a taxpayer's refund check because of a fee dispute. However, a tax preparer is not required to file a client's tax return without first obtaining payment.

**44. The answer is B.** If an e-file hardship waiver is denied, there is an administrative appeal available. Tax return preparers may request a hardship waiver from the e-file requirement by using **Form 8944,** *Preparer e-file Hardship Waiver Request.* **Form 8944** generally must be submitted to the IRS no later than February 15 of the year for which a waiver is being requested.

**45. The answer is D.** The taxpayer may not designate refunds for Direct Deposit to credit card accounts. Taxpayers often elect the Direct Deposit option because it is the fastest way of receiving refunds. Providers must accept any Direct Deposit election to any eligible financial institution designated by the taxpayer. The taxpayer may designate refunds to savings, checking, share draft, or consumer asset accounts (for example, IRA or money market accounts). For more information, see **Publication 1345**, *Handbook for Authorized IRS e-file Providers of Individual Income Tax Returns.*

**46. The answer is B.** Any tax return preparer who fails to comply with due diligence requirements for the EITC can be liable for a penalty of $500 for each failure. The penalty increased from $100 to $500 per return in 2011.

**47. The answer is C.** A hard copy (paper copy) is not required. The preparer must provide a complete copy of the return to the taxpayer. Preparers may provide this copy in any media, including electronic, that is acceptable to both the taxpayer and the preparer. The copy need not contain the Social Security Number of the paid preparer. A complete copy of a taxpayer's return includes **Form 8453** and other documents that the preparer cannot electronically transmit, when applicable, as well as the electronic portion of the return. For more information, see **Publication 1345**, *Handbook for Authorized IRS e-file Providers of Individual Income Tax Returns.*

**48. The answer is C.** Private Letter Rulings are written decisions by the Internal Revenue Service in response to a taxpayer's written request for guidance on a particular tax issue. Private Letter Rulings become public record once issued; all of the taxpayer's personal information is removed.

**49. The answer is C.** The Tax Court may impose sanctions of up to $25,000 on those who misuse their right to a court review merely to file a frivolous argument. If the Tax Court determines that the case is intended primarily to cause a delay or that the taxpayer's position is groundless, the court may award a penalty of up to $25,000 against the individual. For more information, see **Publication 5,** *Your Appeal Rights and How to Prepare a Protest If You Don't Agree.*

**50. The answer is A.** In tax disputes involving $50,000 or less, taxpayers may choose to use the IRS small tax case procedure.

**51. The answer is C.** There are three types of Treasury regulations: legislative, interpretive, and procedural. There is no such thing as a "Congressional regulation" issued by the Treasury Department.

**52. The answer is B.** If an Authorized IRS e-file Provider uses direct mail, e-mail, fax communications, or other distribution methods to advertise, the Provider must retain a copy, as well as a list or other description of the firms, organizations, or individuals to whom the communication was sent, and provide it to the IRS upon request until the end of the calendar year following the date sent. The preparer must keep a copy of the advertisement and provide it to the IRS upon request. Copies must be retained until the end of the calendar year following the last transmission or use. For more information, see **Publication 3112**, *IRS e-file Application and Participation*.

**53. The answer is A.** Rejected electronic individual income tax return data can be corrected and retransmitted without new signatures or authorizations if changes do not differ from the amount on the original electronic return by more than $50 to "total income" or "AGI," or more than $14 to "total tax," "federal income tax withheld," "refund," or "amount you owe." The preparer must give taxpayers copies of the new electronic return data. For more information, see **Publication 1345**, *Handbook for Authorized IRS e-file Providers of Individual Income Tax Returns.*

**54. The answer is D.** The IRS may delay refunds for a number of reasons, including the following:

- Errors in Direct Deposit information (refunds then sent by check);
- Financial institution refusals of Direct Deposits (refunds then sent by check) or delays in crediting the Direct Deposit to the taxpayer's account;
- Estimated tax payments differing from the amount reported on the tax return (for example, fourth quarter payments not yet on file when return data is transmitted);
- Bankruptcy;
- Inappropriate claims for the Earned Income Tax Credit; or

- Recertification to claim the Earned Income Tax Credit.

When a delay occurs, the IRS sends the taxpayer a letter explaining the delay and how to resolve the issue. For more information, see **Publication 1345**, *Handbook for Authorized IRS e-file Providers of Individual Income Tax Returns.*

**55. The answer is B.** If the IRS rejects the electronic portion of a taxpayer's individual income tax return for processing and the Electronic Return Originator cannot rectify the reason for the rejection, the ERO must take reasonable steps to inform the taxpayer of the rejection within 24 hours. When the ERO advises the taxpayer that it has not filed the return, the ERO must provide the taxpayer with the reject code(s) accompanied by an explanation. If the taxpayer chooses not to have the electronic portion of the return corrected and transmitted to the IRS, or if the IRS cannot accept the return for processing, the taxpayer must file a paper return. For more information, see **Publication 1345**, *Handbook for Authorized IRS e-file Providers of Individual Income Tax Returns.*

**56. The answer is A.** A late payment on an installment agreement will generate an automatic 30-day notice that the agreement is terminated, which allows the IRS time to make changes to the installment agreement.

**57. The answer is A.** The ethics requirement for the Enrolled Agent license renewal is a minimum of two hours of ethics per year, so Francisco has not fulfilled his ethics requirement. Section 10.6(e)(2)(ii) requires a minimum of 16 hours of continuing education credit per year, with at least two hours devoted to ethics. If a preparer takes more than two hours of ethics in a single year, the extra ethics hours can count toward the overall minimum requirement. The ethics requirement is in effect every single year.

**58. The answer is C.** Natalie does NOT have to fulfill the overall 72 hours of CPE required during an enrollment cycle since she was only an Enrolled Agent for two years. For renewal purposes, the annual CPE requirements only apply for the years in which someone was an Enrolled Agent. CPE is not required for those years prior to becoming an Enrolled Agent. An EA who receives initial enrollment during an enrollment cycle must complete two CPE hours for each month enrolled during the enrollment cycle. Enrollment for any part of a month is considered enrollment for the entire month.

**59. The answer is B.** The tax preparer may not cash or endorse a taxpayer's refund check. A $500 penalty may be imposed on a return preparer who endorses or negotiates a refund check issued to any taxpayer. This penalty applies even if the taxpayer gives his permission. The prohibition on return preparers negotiating a refund check is limited to a refund check for returns they prepared. For more information, see **Publication 1345**, *Handbook for Authorized IRS e-file Providers of Individual Income Tax Returns.*

**60. The answer is A.** A Refund Anticipation Loan (RAL) is an agreement between a taxpayer and a lender. An RAL is money borrowed by a taxpayer from a lender based on the taxpayer's anticipated income tax refund. The IRS is not involved in or responsible for RALs or other financial products. For more information, see **Publication 1345**, *Handbook for Authorized IRS e-file Providers of Individual Income Tax Returns.*

**61. The answer is B.** A taxpayer can obtain a copy of the actual return and all attachments filed with the IRS for an earlier year by using Form 4506. The taxpayer will be charged a fee for a copy of the return, which must be submitted along with Form 4506.

**62. The answer is A.** A tax preparer may NOT charge a fee based on the percentage of the refund for preparing a Refund Anticipation Loan application. If Providers advertise the availability of an RAL or financial product, the Provider and financial institution must clearly refer to the funds they advance as a loan or other financial product, not as a refund. The advertisement on an RAL or other financial product must be easy to identify and in readable print. For more information, see **Publication 1345**, *Handbook for Authorized IRS e-file Providers of Individual Income Tax Returns.*

**63. The answer is A.** A family member can represent members of his or her immediate family. Immediate family means a spouse, child, parent, brother, or sister of the individual. Because of their special relationship, family members can represent a taxpayer and practice before the IRS, provided they present satisfactory identification and proof of authority to do so. In this case, the mother would need a signed **Form 2848** with the signature of her child.

**64. The answer is B.** The statutory notice of deficiency, the "90-day letter," gives the taxpayer 90 days to file a petition in the United States Tax Court challenging the proposed deficiency. A taxpayer has 150 days if his address is outside of the country on the day the notice of deficiency is mailed.

**65. The answer is C.** The confidentiality privilege does NOT extend to any administrative proceeding with any other federal agency. This privilege applies only to tax advice given to the taxpayer by a federally authorized tax practitioner (EA, CPA, or attorney). The confidentiality protection applies to communications that would be considered privileged if they were between the taxpayer and an attorney and that relate to:

- Non-criminal tax matters before the IRS, or
- Non-criminal tax proceedings brought in federal court by or against the United States.

This confidentiality privilege does NOT apply to tax shelter opinions or criminal matters.

**66. The answer is D.** A Registered Tax Return Preparer is eligible to represent a taxpayer only about a tax liability arising from a tax return prepared for that individual. An unenrolled individual who signs a return as its preparer may act as the taxpayer's representative if accompanied by the taxpayer. Anyone can appear as a witness before the IRS. A Registered Tax Return Preparer is NOT allowed to receive tax refund checks on the client's behalf. For more information, see **Publication 470**, *Limited Practice Without Enrollment.*

**67. The answer is C.** A Registered Tax Return Preparer is allowed an extension of time to file a tax return. The following acts are beyond the scope of the Registered Tax Return Preparer:

- Executing claims for refund
- Receiving checks in payment of any refund of IRS taxes, penalties, or interest
- Executing consents to extend the statute of limitations to collect tax
- Executing closing agreements with respect to a tax liability or specific matter
- Executing waivers of restriction on assessment or collection of a deficiency in tax

The Registered Tax Return Preparer is NOT able to:

- Negotiate payment arrangements
- Argue the validity of the assessment
- Request extensions on collection or assessment deadlines (an unenrolled preparer may file an extension of time to file a tax return)
- Request adjustments to an account
- Represent taxpayers with regard to a tax return they have not prepared

For more information, see **Publication 470**, *Limited Practice Without Enrollment*.

**68. The answer is B.** Providers may not base their fees on a percentage of the refund amount or compute their fees using any figure from tax returns.

**69. The answer is C.** Barbara has a right to appeal the judge's decision. If a practitioner fails to respond to an initial complaint, the failure constitutes an admission of guilt and a waiver of the hearing. The administrative law judge may make a decision on the case by default without a hearing or further procedure. During a hearing, the practitioner may appear in person, or be represented by an attorney or another practitioner. The Director of the OPR may be represented by an attorney or other employee of the IRS. For more information, see **Circular 230**.

**70. The answer is A.** The practitioner may file an appeal to the judge's decision with the Secretary of the Treasury, and not to the OPR. An administrative law judge presides over the hearing on a complaint for censure, suspension, or disbarment. After a decision for disbarment has been made, the tax practitioner has a right to appeal. For more information, see **Circular 230.**

**71. The answer is D.** The IRS has issued regulations regarding covered opinions, which were formerly known as "tax shelter opinions." This relates to the advice a practitioner gives a client regarding a tax shelter. The **Circular 230** requirements apply to all written forms of federal tax advice, and there are strict rules regarding the written advice about a tax shelter. A tax shelter is a technique or arrangement that allows one to legally reduce or avoid tax liabilities. The IRS monitors very closely for abusive tax shelters. Higher communication standards exist for covered opinions. An example of written advice that does NOT qualify as a "covered opinion" includes:

- Advice from in-house employees to their employers.
- Written advice solely for one taxpayer after the taxpayer has already filed a tax return.
- Written advice that does not resolve a federal tax issue in the taxpayer's favor. This is also called "negative advice," wherein an advisor tells a client a transaction will not provide the purported tax benefit.
- Written advice regarding qualified plans, state and local bonds, or SEC-filed documents.
- Any written advice if the practitioner is reasonably expected to provide subsequent written advice that satisfies the covered opinion requirements [IR-2005-59].

The penalties for promoting abusive tax shelters are severe. In addition to monetary penalties, a practitioner can be permanently disbarred, censured, or suspended. For more information, see **Circular 230.**

**72. The answer is D.** An IRS power of attorney ends upon death. For more information, see **Circular 230.**

**73. The answer is D.** An Electronic Return Originator (ERO) originates the electronic submission of returns it either prepares or collects from taxpayers who want to e-file their returns. An ERO originates the electronic submission by:

- Electronically sending the return to a Transmitter that transmits the return to the IRS;
- Directly transmitting the return to the IRS; or
- Providing a return to an Intermediate Service Provider for processing prior to transmission to the IRS.

For more information, see **Publication 1345**, *Handbook for Authorized IRS e-file Providers of Individual Income Tax Returns.*

**74. The answer is D.** Generally, confidential taxpayer information can only be disclosed upon a taxpayer's written authorization. A power of attorney is not required in some situations when dealing with the IRS. The following situations do not require a power of attorney:

- Providing information to the IRS
- Disclosure pursuant to a court order
- Authorizing the disclosure of tax return information through Form 8821
- Allowing the IRS to discuss return information with a third party designee
- Allowing a tax matters partner or person (TMP) to perform acts for the partnership
- Allowing the IRS to discuss return information with a fiduciary
- Representing a taxpayer through a non-written (oral) consent

**75. The answer is A.** Robin may represent both of her clients so long as the conflict of interest is disclosed in writing to both parties and both parties agree. Circular 230 does not ban practitioners from representing clients with conflicts of interest. However, the regulations do require practitioners to obtain written consent to the representation from each affected client. For more information, see **Circular 230**.

**76. The answer is A.** Enrolled Agents must renew their enrollment status every three years. As part of the application process, the IRS checks the candidate's filing history to verify that he has filed and paid all federal taxes on time.

**77. The answer is D.** Not receiving a renewal form is not a valid excuse for a CPE waiver. A waiver of CPE requirements may be requested in extraordinary circumstances. The discretion to grant a waiver lies in the hands of the Office of Professional Responsibility. Qualifying circumstances include:

- Health issues
- Active deployment for military personnel
- Absence from the United States for employment or other reasons
- Other reasons on a case-by-case basis

The request for a waiver must be accompanied by appropriate documentation, such as medical records or military paperwork. If the request is denied, the Enrolled Agent will be placed on the inactive roster. If the request is accepted, the individual will receive an enrollment card reflecting his renewal.

**78. The answer is C. Form 8821** is not sufficient for representation work. **Form 8821,** *Tax Information Authorization*, is an information request form only that authorizes the disclosure of tax information.

**79. The answer is C.** The Taxpayer Advocate Service is an independent organization within the IRS whose employees assist taxpayers who are experiencing economic harm, who are seeking help in resolving tax problems that have not been resolved through normal channels, or who believe that an IRS system or procedure is not working as it should.

**80. The answer is C.** Generally, installment agreements cannot be entered into unless the agreement provides for full payment of the entire tax liability (including interest and penalties) within the earlier of five years or the Collection Statute Expiration Date (Internal Revenue Manual, 4.20.4.2). ***NOTE:** A request for an installment agreement *cannot be turned down* if the tax owed is not more than $10,000 and all three of the following apply:

- During the past five tax years, a taxpayer (and spouse if filing a joint return) have timely filed all income tax returns and paid any income tax due, and have not entered into an installment agreement for payment of income tax.
- The IRS determines that a taxpayer cannot pay the tax owed in full when it is due, after the IRS is provided information it needs to make that determination.
- A taxpayer agrees to pay the full amount he owes within three years and to comply with the tax laws while the agreement is in effect.

**81. The answer is D.** The IRS is not required to comply with all FOIA requests. The IRS may withhold an IRS record that falls under one of the FOIA's nine statutory exemptions or by one of three exclusions under the Act. The exemptions protect against the disclosure of information that would harm the following: national security, the privacy of individuals, the proprietary interests of business, the functioning of the government, and other important recognized interests. For more information, see *The IRS Guide to the Freedom of Information Act.*

**82. The answer is B.** A practitioner may publish and advertise a fee schedule. A practitioner must adhere to the published fee schedule for at least 30 calendar days after it is published. For more information, see **Circular 230**.

**83. The answer is A.** The IRS is not bound to follow the decision of every court case. If courts decide against the IRS position on an issue, the IRS will sometimes issue a statement saying that it disagrees or *non-acquiesces* to the court's decision. This means that the IRS may choose to ignore the decision of the court and continue with its regular policies regarding the litigated issue. The IRS is not bound to change its regulations due to a loss in court. The only exception to this rule is the U.S. Supreme Court, whose decisions the IRS is obligated to follow. The IRS publishes its acquiescence and non-acquiescence in the Internal Revenue Bulletin, and then in the Cumulative Bulletin. The IRS does not announce acquiescence or non-acquiescence in every case. Sometimes the IRS's position is withheld.

**84. The answer is B.** The mission of the Office of Professional Responsibility establishes and enforces consistent standards of competence, integrity, and conduct for tax professionals and other individuals and groups covered by IRS **Circular 230.** Answer "C" is incorrect because it is the mission statement for the IRS Small Business Division. Answer "D" is incorrect because it is the IRS's main mission statement.

**85. The answer is B.** Taxpayers may rely on Revenue Rulings as official IRS guidance on an issue. A taxpayer may use a Revenue Ruling as guidance in order to make a decision regarding taxable income, deductions, and also how to avoid certain IRS penalties. Revenue Rulings may be challenged in court. Revenue Rulings are official IRS interpretations and the IRS is bound by them, but the courts are not.

**86. The answer is D.** The OPR can issue a notice for judicial proceedings for censure, suspension, or disbarment. Criminal penalties may be imposed on a tax preparer for fraudulent activity, but the IRS refers criminal activity to the Department of Justice for prosecution.

**87. The answer is C.** The jurisdiction of the Tax Court does not include employment, wagering, and certain excise taxes. The jurisdiction of the Tax Court includes:

- Income tax, estate tax, and gift tax
- Worker classification
- Innocent spouse claims
- Liens and levies
- Awards of administrative costs
- Enforcement of overpayments
- Redetermination of interest
- Modification of estate tax decision
- Litigation costs awards
- Abatement of interest

**88. The answer is D.** The date of filing is not required. However, it is necessary to state the year or periods involved, such as "2010-2011 tax years." An IRS power of attorney must contain:

- The type of tax and the tax years covered by the power of attorney
- The name and address of the representative
- The name and Social Security Number of the taxpayer
- The signatures of the representative and the taxpayer

The IRS will not accept a power of attorney if it does not contain all the information listed above.

**89. The answer is B.** A paid preparer is required by law to sign the return and fill in the preparer areas of the form. The preparer must also include his PTIN on the return. Although the preparer signs the return, the client is ultimately responsible for the accuracy of every item on it. In addition, the preparer must give the taxpayer a copy of the return.

**90. The answer is C.** There is no requirement that the practitioner have a permanent business location outside his home. In fact, many e-file providers work exclusively from a home office. An Authorized IRS e-file Provider is a business authorized by the IRS to participate in IRS e-file. The business may be a sole proprietorship, partnership, or corporation. The applicant must:

- Be a United States citizen or a legal U.S. alien lawfully admitted for permanent residence;
- Be at least 21 years old as of the date of application; and
- Meet applicable state and local licensing and/or bonding requirements for the preparation and collection of tax returns.

**91. The answer is E.** The IRS must give a taxpayer reasonable notice before contacting other persons about his tax issues. This provision does not apply:

- To any pending criminal investigation
- When providing notice would jeopardize collection of any tax liability
- When providing notice may result in reprisal against any person
- When the taxpayer authorized the contact

For more information, see **Publication 556**, *Examination of Returns, Appeal Rights, and Claims for Refund.*

**92. The answer is D.** Communications about the promotion of a person's participation in a tax shelter are not covered by the confidentiality privilege. A tax shelter is any plan designed for the avoidance of tax. For more information, see **Circular 230.**

**93. The answer is A.** A taxpayer is allowed to record the examination interview. The request to record the interview should be made in writing. The taxpayer or representative must notify the examiner ten days in advance and bring his own recording equipment. The IRS also can record an interview. For more information, see **Publication 556**, *Examination of Returns, Appeal Rights, and Claims for Refund.*

**94. The answer is D.** Most cases that are *not docketed* in any court qualify for fast track mediation. Mediation can take place at a conference a taxpayer requests with a supervisor, or later. The process involves an Appeals Officer who has been trained in mediation. Certain matters are excluded from fast track mediation. They include:

- Issues for which there is no legal precedent
- Issues where the courts have rendered opposing or differing decisions in different jurisdictions
- Industry Specialization Program issues
- Collection Appeals Program cases
- Automated Collection System cases
- Constitutional law issues

For more information, see **Publication 3605**, *Fast Track Mediation-A Process for Prompt Resolution of Tax Issues.*

**95. The answer is A.** Penny may appeal the termination of her installment agreement. If she appeals within a 30-day period after the termination, the IRS will be prohibited from levying until her appeal is completed. For more information, see **Publication 1660**, *Collection Appeal Rights.*

**96. The answer is D.** A taxpayer cannot appeal a CAP decision to the court. Once Appeals makes a decision regarding the case, that decision is binding on both the taxpayer and the IRS. A taxpayer cannot obtain judicial review of the decision following a CAP hearing. For more information, see **Publication 1660**, *Collection Appeal Rights*.

**97. The answer is B.** An IRS interview must be suspended when the taxpayer clearly requests the right to consult with a representative. Throughout the examination process, the taxpayer can act on his own behalf or have someone represent him. The taxpayer is not required to be present if the representative is a federally authorized practitioner (Enrolled Agent, CPA, or attorney). The taxpayer is also not required to be present if the representative is one of the other qualified unenrolled individuals listed in **Circular 230**, such as a family member or an employee representing an employer. For more information, see **Publication 556**, *Examination of Returns, Appeal Rights, and Claims for Refund.*

**98. The answer is A.** A CP-2000 shows proposed changes to a taxpayer's income tax return. A CP-2000 notice is not a bill. It is a request for verification of the income, credits, and deductions reported on the tax return. A CP-2000 is a proposal that offers the taxpayer an opportunity to disagree, partially agree, or agree with the proposed changes. The taxpayer must respond within 30 days of the date of the notice (or 60 days if living outside the United States). If the IRS does not hear from the taxpayer within the 30 or 60 day period, a statutory notice of deficiency will be issued and additional interest will be charged.

**99. The answer is C.** In most cases, tax returns can be audited for up to three years after filing. However, the IRS may audit for up to six years if there is substantial unreported income.

**100. The answer is C.** Taxpayers are given ten days from the date of a rejected return to resubmit the return, even if the submission is made after the due date of the return. The "transmission perfection period" is NOT an extension of time to file; it is additional time to correct errors in the electronic file. When a previously rejected electronic return is "accepted" by the IRS within the ten-day transmission perfection period, it will be deemed to have been received on the date of the first reject that occurred within that ten-day period.

# The Enrolled Agent Tax Consulting Practice Guide

*Learn How to Develop, Market, and Operate a Profitable Tax and IRS Representation Practice*

Available as a Kindle edition, paperback, and a Nook edition

# About the Authors

Collette Szymborski is a Certified Public Accountant and the managing partner of Elk Grove CPA Accountancy Corporation. She specializes in the taxation of corporations, individuals, and exempt entities. Elk Grove CPA also does estate and elder care planning.

Richard Gramkow is an Enrolled Agent with over fifteen years of experience in various areas of taxation. He holds a Master's Degree in Taxation from Rutgers University and is currently a Tax Manager for a publicly held Fortune 500 company in the New York metropolitan area.

Christy Pinheiro is an Enrolled Agent, Accredited Business Accountant, and writer. Christy was an accountant for two private CPA firms and for the State of California before going into private practice. She is a member of the California Society of Enrolled Agents and National Association of Tax Professionals.

15449424R00111

Made in the USA
Lexington, KY
29 May 2012